AF521334

INDIA ASPIRES

Nitin Gadkari
as told to Tuhin A Sinha

India Aspires

Redefining Politics of Development

wisdom tree

© Nitin Gadkari, 2013

First published 2013
Reprinted 2014, 2015

All rights reserved. No part of this book may be reproduced, stored in a retrieval system or transmitted in any form or by any means—electronic, mechanical, photocopying, recording or otherwise—without the prior permission of the author and the publisher.

Although every effort has been made to ensure that the information in this book was correct at the time of going to press, the authors and publisher hereby disclaim any liability resulting from the use of any information contained herein.

ISBN 978-81-8328-455-4

Published by

Wisdom Tree
4779/23, Ansari Road
Darya Ganj, New Delhi-110002
Ph.: 23247966/67/68
wisdomtreebooks@gmail.com

Printed in India

Contents

An idea that is developed and
put into action is more important
than an idea that exists only
as an idea.

—Gautam Buddha

ONE

Reviving a Dream

It was on a mundane winter evening of December 2009 that I received a call from the central leadership of my party. Nothing, absolutely nothing, had given me any hint of the surprise that was in store: I was asked to take up the responsibility of leading the Bharatiya Janata Party (BJP) as its president.

I couldn't believe it at first. As president of the Maharashtra BJP, and with no experience of national-level politics, I was pretty content with the work I was doing in my home state. I had no real aspirations to be in Delhi. Besides, the party wasn't in the best of health. After losing the 2009 Lok Sabha elections, there was an urgent need to regain lost ground. Why did the party, then, choose me for the post over some of our senior leaders? To be honest, I had my doubts about taking up the mammoth responsibility.

Undecided, I went to meet Atal Bihari Vajpayeeji, whom I hold in great reverence. He was unwell and not in a position to speak. But he made a sign that drove away all my hesitation.

He raised his right arm in a gesture of blessing. And, at that very moment, all my doubts and fears were allayed. I couldn't say no to his bidding. I told myself, I will go the extra mile to live up to the faith that was being reposed in me.

On 19 December 2009, I took charge as the ninth president of the BJP, a post that had been graced in the past by Vajpayeeji and Lal Krishna Advaniji. For someone who has always thought of himself as an ordinary worker of the party, I was most humbled to take over as its president. That night, I experienced a wide range of emotions as I reflected upon my political journey of more than three decades.

I was born into an agricultural family in the early years of India's Independence. Like millions of other families, we basked in the hopes and aspirations of our young nation. I have always believed that one's parents, and especially the childhood years, leave a big influence on one's personality. It was my mother I always looked up to.

Despite owning some farming land and a house, the financial condition of my family was not comfortable. This, however, did not prevent my mother from helping the needy. She would always be the first one to help a neighbour in times of distress or would go out of her way to help the sick. As a child, I often wondered why my mother had to worry so much about other people's well-being. But, as I grew up, I realised I had inherited her large-heartedness. Even in times of financial crisis, I would end up helping friends who were worse off, often upsetting my wife in the process. Somehow, bringing joy to others' lives filled me with a rare sense of satisfaction—it was a habit and philosophy that I inherited, practised and held throughout.

In my early years, I have seen members of my family struggle to make ends meet. My two elder sisters, who were married off early, would arduously accumulate 25 and 50 paise coins to buy me a gift during Diwali. Knowing their hardship, I felt guilty accepting those gifts. That, however, made me realise the worth of every penny that I earned later. Moreover, it kept me grounded. It made me acutely aware that there were others who weren't as lucky as I was. Thus, somewhere, I became conditioned to be content with as much as would fulfil my necessities for a decent living. Instead of maximising my earnings and profits, my interest was to share the extra pie with the lesser privileged around me.

During my college years, when I saw the dedicated volunteers of the Rashtriya Swayamsevak Sangh (RSS) cadre in Nagpur working towards shaping the future of the nation with the same objectives as I had—only on a much larger scale—it was but natural for me to be drawn to them. Thanks to my early orientation, my focus in politics was, and has always been, to improve the living conditions of the downtrodden and that gave me a common ground with the RSS. I got involved very closely with the RSS and the Akhil Bharatiya Vidyarthi Parishad (ABVP), an all-India student organisation that has worked extensively for social causes. Thus, I took to social work in a big way. I was particularly inspired by RSS founder KB Hedgewar's ideals of humanity and nation building.

In the Seventies though, the optimism of the initial years of Independence was replaced with chaos and uncertainty. It was also around then that we realised there was perhaps something terribly amiss with our approach towards development.

The honest quest for innovative solutions to people's most basic needs, is what ought to be the driving force of a politician's life. The need of the hour was to identify and embark upon a course correction, so that we set our failures aside and sincerely endeavour to transform our country into the land of glory which she was always meant to be.

Our progress had been lopsided, with the result that amenities, especially in rural India, remained woefully inadequate, while unemployment across the country became a scourge. Disappointment built up in various sections of society. This, unfortunately, coincided with a phase when the then prime minister, Indira Gandhi, had become increasingly intolerant of the Opposition. Instead of addressing the problems confronting the nation, she focussed her energies on suppressing the Opposition. It was in this situation that, on 12 June 1975, Justice Jagmohanlal Sinha of the Allahabad High Court passed a ruling indicting Mrs Gandhi for misuse of government machinery for her election campaign. The court declared her election null and void and unseated her from the Lok Sabha. Nationwide protests led by Jaiprakash Narayan, Morarji Desai and other leaders followed, demanding the resignation of Mrs Gandhi. Confronted with this growing threat to her position, Indira Gandhi retaliated by hastily imposing 'internal emergency' in the country.

The imposition of Emergency only precipitated the angst of a betrayed nation. The extent of excesses carried out by the then government shook me out of my comfort zone. As a student, I aggressively campaigned against the Emergency.

Certain political developments leave a strong impression on an individual's life; I realised that the Emergency had changed my approach to life. Had there been no Emergency, I would have gone on to practice law. Emergency made me conscious of the need to fight for the democratic rights of citizens and also to safeguard the democratic system of governance in India. No regime, under any circumstance whatsoever, has the right to suppress the fundamental rights conferred on the citizens under a country's Constitution. The Emergency, thus, was a turning point in my life. My active participation in politics began in those days and there has been no looking back since.

An enduring feature which guides my political life has been to try and improve the life of the underprivileged. *Antyodaya*, as we call it, stands for eradication of abject poverty, provision of basic necessities to every Indian family and ensuring that the last man in society gets the first opportunity to rise in life. This is what Swami Vivekananda, Mahatma Gandhi, Pandit Deendayal Upadhyaya and other saintly figures in India had emphasised. I wish to especially mention Gandhi's 'principle of trusteeship' and Pandit Upadhyaya's concept of 'integral humanism' as philosophies that inspire my thought process.

What our leaders had envisioned for free India has not happened. The tribals in the Sironcha region of Maharashtra still consume crushed red ants, instead of salt. Can there be a sadder commentary on the way certain regions have been consistently neglected since Independence?

The biggest impediment in our path towards equitable prosperity has been the sheer absence of political will. The inertia or inability of our political class to engineer changes in the existing order has led to stagnation, where even smaller developing countries have surged ahead of us.

The first opportunity to try and change an outdated system came my way in 1995. As a minister of the Public Works Department (PWD) in Maharashtra, I was dismayed by the poor road connectivity to villages, even after five decades of Independence. One of the first tasks that I undertook was to provide all-weather roads to the 13,736 villages in Maharashtra. All the projects that I undertook as PWD minister were carried out with utmost transparency, adhering to the highest standards of integrity.

My quest for solutions led me to adopt the Public Private Partnership (PPP) model, popularly known as Build Operate Transfer (BOT), for executing several development projects. Later, the same model was employed elsewhere for what we see today as the Golden Quadrilateral and many roads built by the National Highway Authority of India (NHAI), the Pradhan Mantri Gram Sadak Yojana and other similar projects. It is my firm belief that unless road connectivity is provided to the most backward villages of the country, *Antyodaya* cannot be realised. I am happy and satisfied that in my tenure as PWD minister, apart from undertaking and executing several difficult projects, in my own small way, I was able to offer a solution to the vexing problem of funding that confronts most infrastructure projects in our country.

We need honest leaders who can take hard decisions. Honest leaders who are indecisive are useless. Dishonest and indecisive leaders are a curse.

Even six and a half decades after India attained freedom, the standard of living for our rural population has not shown any significant improvement. It has been my strong belief that unless the purchasing power of farmers is increased, society will not progress as a whole. With this view, in 2000, I launched the Purti Group, which took up sugarcane farming, sugar production and co-generation of power using renewable energy sources. The organisation's diversified status originates from its strategy, aimed at creating multiple drivers of growth for farmers and unemployed youth. I am happy that this 'social entrepreneurship' initiative has helped in improving the lives of farmers in the Vidarbha region of Maharashtra. We need many such social entrepreneurship initiatives in each of the 645 districts of our country.

When I became the party president, I was entrusted with

a huge responsibility. The BJP has always believed in the principle 'nation first, party next and self last'. We have always placed national interests above everything else. The Congress, on the other hand, did just the opposite. I am saddened by the sheer mediocrity in our governance standards every time a Congress government is in power. Sadly, in the last six and a half decades of our Independence, the Congress has been in power for almost fifty-seven years.

In 1947, when we emerged as an independent nation after centuries of foreign misrule, we had a magnificent opportunity to transform our nation into the world's most progressive and powerful country. To my understanding, India's multiple failures today are the result of a chain of political blunders that have taken place ever since.

The opportunity which came our way at the time of Independence was botched up by the leadership that got the reins of free India. The principal factor responsible for this act of squandering was our first prime minister's flawed understanding of the concept of development. 'Nehruvian Socialism', as we know it today, empowered state institutions to such a disproportionate level that it became the biggest impediment to our growth and progress as a nation. One, despite enormous expenditure, there was only so much that the state alone could do, given the size of our nation and our population. Two, indiscriminate patronage of the state killed entrepreneurship and deprived us of a crucial competitive edge that we could have gained otherwise. Three, even decades after attaining sovereignty, while some of the other developing countries prospered at a brisk pace, large parts of our country grappled with an acute deficit of multiple kinds—electricity, water, education, infrastructure. This rendered all our poverty alleviation initiatives ineffective.

As a result, we never had a concrete, holistic, well-rounded agricultural policy. This, despite the fact that more than 85 per cent of our population lived in rural areas in 1947. While the state invested considerably in steel plants, aviation and railways, basic issues like irrigation, health and connectivity in rural areas were consistently ignored.

Over the years, the poverty alleviation measures have not benefitted everyone equally—according to National Council for Enterprises in the Unorganized Sector (NCEUS) data, 33 per cent of our population earns less than ₹70 a day whereas more than 16 per cent earns less than ₹20 a day. In any case, the government's decision to define the poverty line at a meagre ₹32 per person per day is shocking.

India certainly deserves better.

In January 2013, after I relinquished the post of BJP president, I had more time to mull over the issues that hold us back as a nation. That is when I decided to revisit some of my thoughts on these issues and the idea of writing a book came up.

There are two primary reasons why I decided to write this book. One, to put into practice what has been my firm belief from the day I joined politics: Politics is an instrument for socio-economic change. It is not about inter-party or intra-party one-upmanship. Neither is this about empty rhetoric or mud-slinging. Constructive politics must transcend the ambitions of ministerial berths and party posts. There is an urgent need to bring back basic social concerns relating to urban infrastructure, rural needs, environment, health etc. to the forefront of our political agenda. If we claim to serve the people, we must be sensitive to what ails them rather than making them subscribe to our selfish political agendas.

Honesty is the biggest capital we must work for. And the honest quest for innovative solutions to our people's most basic needs is what ought to be the driving force of a politician's life. This book is my attempt to reinstate this belief in India's political culture.

Secondly, this is my attempt to offer dynamic and tested solutions to the multiple problems that plague us today.

This book is a humble offering to my countrymen. It comes from a man who does not consider himself erudite in a country known for its exceptional scholars. Rather, I simply believe in the enormous power of political initiatives. I believe that right-minded, honest and decisive leadership can still rectify the flaws that hold us back as a nation.

India, with the dual advantage of her rich natural resources and technological advancements, can emerge to be the world's most powerful nation. We, the present and future generations of this country, have in our hands, an opportunity to revive, engineer and fulfil that elusive Indian dream.

We are responsible for what we are and whatever we wish ourselves to be, we have the power to make ourselves. If what we are now has been the result of our past actions, it certainly follows that whatever we wish to be in future can be produced by our present action.

—Swami Vivekananda

TWO

New Agenda for National Politics

February, 2010:

There are moments in one's life when words fail to adequately express one's emotions. It happened with me when I addressed the enthusiastic delegates of my party at our national council meet in Indore after becoming party president. My focus, prior to becoming the president of the BJP, had only been Maharashtra. I had not even thought of shifting to national politics. And here I was, addressing *karyakartas* (party workers) from across the country. It was an overwhelming experience, to say the least. I could see in the party workers, the same commitment to serve the country that I had witnessed at the founding conference of the BJP in Mumbai in December 1980. I had attended that session as a young party volunteer.

I was humbled by the enormous trust and confidence that

the national council had placed in me. I had never in my life expected that I would be called upon to serve as president of this great party. I know it and I say it without any hesitation, that there is no dearth of persons with requisite leadership quality in our party and there are many other leaders who, too, could have shouldered this responsibility. Yet, the party leadership elected me to occupy this position. I, as a disciplined soldier of the party, accepted it with a sense of mission.

My election as the party president only underlined the importance of a party worker, as the honour had been bestowed on somebody who was basically a party worker. I didn't have a famous surname. Neither did I belong to a political family. I was born in an ordinary family in Nagpur. I learnt my first lessons in patriotism and social service in the RSS and the ABVP. My election as the president also underlined the fact that the BJP offers equal opportunities for growth to one and all, with merit being the only determinant of the positions given to its workers.

Being the president of a political party is like being the captain of a team. As such, the president's perception, of what the party ought to represent and what it should stand for, plays a pivotal role in influencing people's perspectives about the party. There are certain things that had endeared me to the Bharatiya Jana Sangh (BJS) and the BJP when I was young. And here, I would like to share with you, my understanding of what sets the BJP apart from any other party in our country.

First and foremost, the BJP is truly a party of grassroots-level activists. If I started off as a ward-level political worker by canvassing for the BJS in my early teens, there is nothing unusual about it. In fact, many of us have started our political career by participating in activities like wall painting and poster pasting at election time or other important events. In fact, because of my bad handwriting, I could never write slogans on the walls. Instead, I would lay out durries at party events.

The journey of my political life is by no means unique. Indeed, all the past presidents of the BJP were committed party workers who hailed from the grassroots. In fact, my becoming the all-India president, only reiterates the importance that we, as a party, attach to the ground-level party worker. The BJP is not a party controlled by a family or a dynasty and this is what distinguishes it from most political parties in India, where the highest office is treated as the birthright of members of a particular family. This is what underscores the party's deeper commitment to the ideals of democracy. This is what we mean when we say that the BJP is a party with a difference.

The BJP's ideals are derived from the vision and sacrifice of two great souls, Dr Syama Prasad Mookerjee and Pandit Deendayal Upadhyaya, who always put the nation first, party next and self last in all their deeds and thoughts.

The lives and teachings of these two legends have inspired us since the beginning of our political journey in 1951, when the BJS was born. Had it not been for the indefatigable efforts of these leaders in laying a strong foundation for our party, the BJP may not have grown to the position of strength that we find it in today.

Dr Mookerjee founded the BJS on 21 October 1951. The party was opposed to religious appeasement in the garb of vote bank politics and favoured free market economics, rather than the Socialist policies pursued by Nehru. The BJS also favoured a uniform civil code governing personal laws for both Hindus and Muslims, wanted to ban cow slaughter and end the special status given to the state of Jammu and Kashmir.

Dr Mookerjee fought valiantly for his beliefs. In 1953, he launched a massive protest against the law that prohibited Indian citizens from settling in Kashmir and mandated that they carry a special permit. He was arrested after crossing the border into Kashmir. Although the permit system was revoked, thanks to his efforts, he died in detention on 23 June 1953, under mysterious circumstances.

I have already spoken of Pandit Deendayal Upadhyaya's philosophy of 'Integral Humanism' earlier. It was he who propounded the thesis that the spirit of nationalism and upliftment of the downtrodden together can evolve a political philosophy that can attract all sections of society. Through his untiring efforts, he developed the BJS as a political party for all patriotic people. The vision of this enlightened duo will continue to guide us forever in our task of nation building.

When the first non-Congress government came to power in 1977, the BJS was an important constituent of the ruling Janta Party coalition. However, with the premature collapse of the government in 1979, many of the BJS leaders felt the need to re-launch the party in a new independent avatar. Hence the BJP was founded in December 1980.

In later years, two other leaders—AB Vajpayee, the founder president of the BJP, and LK Advani, who has made a seminal contribution to the growth of the party, led us on the path chalked out by Dr Mookerjee and Pandit Upadhyaya.

Vajpayeeji's legacy of wise and balanced approach to national affairs, his widely adored personality and his enormous contribution to nation building as one of India's best prime ministers, make him a source of strength and pride for the BJP. It is my good fortune that I can count on the wise guidance of Advaniji. As someone whose own political journey began with the formation of the BJS, and who has witnessed and participated in almost all the major developments in national politics in the past six decades, Advaniji is a rare link who connects the past and the present of the BJP. His dedication, selflessness and tireless service make him a leader to emulate for the younger generation of political activists.

Two other leaders whom party activists will always remain indebted to are Kushabhau Thakre and Vijayaraje Scindia. Right from the early days of the BJS, these two leaders worked relentlessly to help the party attain the position of strength which it did in the late nineties; Kushabhau Thakre served as the president of the party between 1998-2000.

What I have imbibed from the great leaders, as well as ideal party workers, is the sheer sense of selflessness towards safeguarding national interests. No other party in India places so much emphasis on national interests. This has been, and will continue to be, our guiding principle. All our party workers must diligently follow this principle; that alone can help us become better servants of the people and make the BJP a better instrument of nation building. We must remember that nationalism is our inspiration and development through good governance for *Antyodaya*, our ultimate goal.

The Challenges

After heading the National Democratic Alliance (NDA) government between 1998-2004, the BJP now has been the country's main opposition party for the last nine years. In these nine years, people have suffered due to the United Progressive Alliance's (UPA) indecisive leadership.

Many of the ambitious projects that we had been working on, like the national river connectivity project, were shelved. At the same time, the government, which is headed by a competent economist, appeared clueless in combating inflation, with the result that prices have continued to soar unabated, adding to the misery of the common man. Worse, the annual growth rate has been falling in recent years. From 9.32 per cent in 2010-11, India recorded an unimpressive annual growth rate of 4.96 per cent in 2012-13 and an even more dismal 4.4 per cent in the first quarter of 2013. Foreign investments have slowed down drastically in the last two years, even as the government looks unprepared to unleash any major reforms. What is worse is that, in the last few months, the value of the rupee against the dollar has been falling consistently. As I write this, the value of the rupee stands at 68 against a dollar whereas, according to data released by the Central Statistics Office on 30 August 2013, the Indian economy grew at just 4.4 per cent between April-June, 2013. This was the lowest quarterly growth rate in four years. Yet, our prime minister and the finance minister remain unfazed and clueless. In this situation, the spectre of increased unemployment looms large over the country.

Given the UPA government's myriad failures, people have huge expectations from us and we must work harder to live up to these expectations.

The BJP today faces stiff challenges which we must candidly admit, objectively understand and resolutely overcome. However, we must not let the challenges before the party cloud our view of the real opportunities that we have. We must strive collectively to overcome the setback of the last Lok Sabha elections and bounce back with renewed vigour. Let us not forget that we are a party which has a presence in all parts of the country—ruling by itself in four states and governing in alliance in Punjab. In five other states, we are the principal opposition party. We have been in power in about twenty states at one point of time or the other. This is the time to build upon what we have achieved so far. There are some states where we are yet to become a significant political force. We must win the confidence of all sections of society in every part of the country and make every effort to give our fellow countrymen what they deserve: Good governance!

As I have mentioned before, safeguarding national interests has always topped our agenda. Helping India regain her lost glory is, thus, our collective national duty. And this we have to do against the backdrop of the transformation that is now taking place in the world order. In the changing world order, we must realise that internal developments within a country are not unaffected by developments in other parts of the world. The global domination by the West, particularly by the United States of America (USA), is rapidly becoming a thing of the past. The recent financial meltdown and economic recession in Western countries should not be seen as a minor downturn. They have had a deep impact on the economic activities of the West. Western countries are waking up to the unsustainability of high-cost, wasteful and excessively consumerist lifestyles—not to speak of the untenable levels of military spending to maintain their global hegemony. Apart from this, they are also battling issues like rising unemployment.

As a consequence, the centre of gravity of the world economic order is irreversibly shifting from the West to Asia. Undoubtedly, China has been a big beneficiary of this change. But the fact that India also can quickly emerge as a major global power is now being recognised by more and more people around the world. No major problem affecting the world—be it climate change, global economic slowdown, restructuring of the global financial architecture, or how to tackle the scourge of international terrorism—can now be discussed without seeking India's participation and cooperation. I regard this change as a historic opportunity for India, perhaps the greatest since Independence. This is the time to rise as a strong and prosperous nation that has a strong voice in the comity of nations.

The Response

The BJP must recognise this opportunity.

We must evolve an appropriate response that reflects in

our political activities, our policies and in the functioning of our governments, including local bodies.

We are an India-first party and strongly believe that the development of the nation is of utmost importance and, hence, we have no hesitation in extending support and cooperation to the Central government and non-BJP governments in various states.

I have always believed that political parties need to show keener interest in international affairs. Our flawed foreign policy has, many a time, been the cause of India not getting its due in international forums.

The emerging challenges across the world call for a common approach through consensus on important strategic issues. While saying this, I would urge the leaders of the UPA to adopt a nationalist approach, based on dialogue and cooperation with the Opposition on all strategic issues affecting the vital interests of the nation. The government failed to do so at the time of forging the Indo-US nuclear deal (2008); and again while evolving India's stand at the Copenhagen Climate Change Summit (2009). It also failed when the financial crisis in the West impacted India's economy severely. Unfortunately, the same attitude of not taking the Opposition into confidence continues with respect to two critical issues that have a direct bearing on the unity, integrity and security of the nation. Incidentally, both have their origin in the grievous mistakes committed by Congress governments in the past. Because of these mistakes, which the Congress leadership of today refuses to acknowledge, India has had to pay a heavy price and suffer hugely for the past several decades.

CHINA

The first concerns India's relations with China. The BJP favours friendly, cordial, neighbourly and cooperative relations with

China, as befits two ancient Asian civilisations. However, now that our neighbour is emerging as a global power, its attitude towards India is far from friendly. Because of China's intransigence, there has been little progress in the talks to resolve the border dispute. China's repeated incursions into Ladakh in the last few months have cast a big question mark over it's intentions, while our External Affairs Minister, Salman Khurshid's pacifist approach has only emboldened the Chinese. At the same time, Beijing's totally untenable and unacceptable claim on Arunachal Pradesh is being frequently expressed in many offensive ways. Our own government has admitted, several times, that China has made incursions into Indian territory in some stretches of the border. This cannot be taken lightly, as the government often seems to be doing. China's growing military presence in India's neighbourhood, including reports of Beijing's plans to set up a military base in Pakistan, is also a matter of concern.

The BJP rightly expects and demands that the government holds appropriate consultations with the Opposition on a strategic approach to India-China relations. We believe that China will appreciate the fact that 2013 is not 1962. Peaceful co-existence is the only way for the two historic civilisations to engage with each other.

Having said that, all efforts must still be made to promote peace and friendship with our Himalayan neighbours. So, when the Central Committee of the ruling Communist Party of China invited me, along with a BJP delegation, on a goodwill visit to China, I happily accepted the invitation. The visit, which took place in January 2011, was aimed at promoting party-to-party contact between the BJP and the Communist Party of China. I studied various path-breaking development initiatives taken by our neighbour. It also gave me the opportunity to discuss the border and other key issues with our counterpart in China.

JAMMU AND KASHMIR

The second important issue is that of Jammu and Kashmir. For all Indians, and especially for BJP workers, Jammu and Kashmir has become the symbol of sacrifice. It was here that Dr Mookerjee dedicated his life for the true spirit of national integration.

With respect to Jammu and Kashmir, the UPA government is heading in the wrong direction, with dangerous implications for the country. It seems to be yielding to external pressures for compromising India's long-held position that the state, including Pak-occupied Kashmir (PoK), is an integral part of India.

Certain controversial remarks made by some Kashmiri leaders in 2010, questioning Kashmir's accession to India, were not even condemned by the UPA government, which raises doubts about its intentions. Equally intriguing was the manner in which the Union Home Ministry had appointed a team of interlocutors comprising journalist Dileep Padgaonkar, educationist Radha Kumar and former information commissioner MM Ansari on 13 October 2010, to hold a sustained dialogue with all sections of society in Jammu and Kashmir and to come up with its recommendations to solve the Kashmir problem. This team released its report on 24 May 2012. It is disconcerting that the report is sympathetic towards the separatists and shows no concern for those who have suffered at the hands of militants. The report unjustifiably calls for a review of all central acts and articles of the Indian Constitution extended to the state after 1952.

Furthermore, it recommends the deletion of the word 'Temporary' from the heading of Article 370 and from the title of Part XXI of the Constitution, and replacing it with the word 'Special' as it has been used for other States under article 371 (Maharashtra and Gujarat); Article 371A (Nagaland); 371B (Assam); 371C (Manipur); 371D and E (Andhra Pradesh);

371F (Sikkim); 371G (Mizoram); 371H (Arunachal Pradesh); 371I (Goa).

The BJP outrightly rejects this biased report. Instead of suggesting ways that would make Jammu and Kashmir's integration with the country more robust, terms like 'autonomy', 'self-rule' and 'independence', which have been generously used in the report, take us back in time. Strangely, while we consider the continuance of Article 370 responsible for the Kashmir problem, the interlocutors have endorsed it strongly. As such, I would consider their recommendations anti-Constitutional.

While the Central government has been generally sympathetic towards the separatists, within the state, the coalition government of National Conference and the Congress takes an even more accommodative approach vis-a-vis Pak-supported separatists. I am constrained to conclude that the UPA government appears to be coming round to the view that Kashmir deserves to be treated separately. From this position, yielding to actual separation is but a step away.

The BJP would like to warn the UPA and caution our countrymen, including right-thinking people within the Congress party and its allies, that the present course of events will lead to the logical culmination of the original blunder committed in 1947, when India had meekly let go of a part of Kashmir, which we today know as Pakistan Occupied Kashmir. We will never let this happen. We are prepared to make any sacrifices for ensuring that Jammu and Kashmir remains an integral part of India. In this context, I reiterate my party's strong opposition to any composite dialogue with Pakistan at this juncture. Besides, the Congress party, which is in power both at the Centre and in Jammu and Kashmir, must take all the necessary steps to ensure the return of lakhs of forcibly displaced Kashmiri Pandits to their own homes, with the guarantee of dignity and security.

SECURITY

The BJP believes that national security, external or internal, is always above narrow political or social considerations. Our party has a proud tradition of supporting the government of the day whenever India's security is endangered. Similarly, when the BJP-led NDA government was in office at the Centre (1999-2004), it actively sought the views and cooperation from other parties in evolving its responses to issues of national security. In our opinion, this healthy tradition should have been pursued by the UPA as well.

In view of the developing security environment in our neighbourhood, India's defence preparedness must not be lowered under any circumstances. On the contrary, there is an urgent need for modernisation and upgradation of our armed forces. Utmost vigilance and more effective strategies are also needed to tackle the twin threats to India's internal security—terrorism and Naxalism. The UPA government's performance in dealing with terrorism in its first stint was absolutely disastrous. Its stubbornness in repealing the Prevention of Terrorism Act (POTA), despite sage counsel to the contrary, only provided a boost to terrorist organisations and led to a rapid increase in terror activities between 2006-08.

After continuously living in denial, the Pak-sponsored 26/11 terrorist attack on Mumbai forced the government to correct some of its mistakes. However, the manner in which the investigation into the 26/11 attacks was carried out, again raised grave doubts. There are reasons to believe that the government was disinterested in probing the local links of the planners and perpetrators of the attacks.

It is sad that the government's weak-kneed approach has already affected the morale of our internal security establishments. According to a written reply submitted by the Minister of State for Home Affairs, Jitendra Singh, in the Rajya Sabha in April 2012, 458 lives were lost in terror attacks in Mumbai alone since 2000. At the same time, in the interiors of Chhattisgarh, Jharkhand, Maharashtra and Odisha (formerly Orissa), several hundreds of lives are lost in Naxal attacks on our security forces and civilians. Whether it is an act of terrorist aggression or Maoist violence, an important question that the nation must debate and come to the right conclusion is this: Whether the people who sacrifice their lives while battling these anti-national elements are entitled to human rights. It is high time the bluff of a section of human rights activists is called.

Even after the 26/11 attack, bomb blasts have continued to take place, albeit with fewer casualties. The bomb blasts in Pune on 13 February 2010, in Mumbai on 13 July 2011, in Pune on 1 August 2012, in Hyderabad on 21 February 2013 and in Bodh Gaya on 7 July 2013, are stark reminders of the fact that pampering of suspected terrorists nullifies the element of deterrence in our internal security regime. Besides, such pampering is also an insult to the memories of those police officers and members of the security forces who have sacrificed their lives fighting terrorism. Some Congress leaders have converted suspected dens of terrorists into places of 'political pilgrimage'. Repeated visits of politicians to those areas have emboldened the enemies of the nation.

Secondly, our diplomatic initiatives with Pakistan lack clarity, consistency and firmness. More than once, in 2013, Indian soldiers have been killed across the LOC without any provocation. The Indian government's reaction, as usual, was weak-kneed. The UPA must realise that, when terror and incursions stalk India, not talking with Pakistan is a legitimate diplomatic option. Unfortunately, the UPA government is not continuing the NDA government's policy of building a broad international consensus against terrorism that could isolate the ideological sponsors of cross-border terrorism. The international community must be made to recognise that Pakistan's ruling political and military establishment rely on terrorism as an instrument of achieving the secession of Kashmir from India. Therefore, any action which appears to be giving Pakistan legitimacy on the Kashmir issue is a sure way of weakening India's battle against terrorism.

Instead of dealing with terrorism with an iron hand, the government is keen on developing absurd terminologies like 'saffron terror'. I wish to emphatically state here, that the BJP never links terrorism with the religious identity of the suspected terrorist. However, the Congress' malicious effort in coining the term 'saffron terror' has inflicted a blow to the secular fabric of our country. Besides, it has weakened our fight against the enemies of our nation. It is really for the people of India to decide whose thought process borders on communal ideology and who is secular in approach.

VOTE BANK POLITICS

Similarly, vote bank politics is also being given a free run in the haste with which both the Congress and the Communists are proceeding to introduce religion-based reservations in education and employment for Muslims. We support every effort for the socio-economic development of our Muslim brethren through greater spread of education. Indeed, their backwardness is an eloquent testimony to how the Congress party has only exploited them for its own political gains. But the concept of religion-based reservations goes against the letter and spirit of the Indian Constitution. Also, it does not even lead to the all-round development of the community as a whole. Rather, it is a divisive move that will harm the unity and integrity of the country in the long run, besides encouraging religious conversions.

The move to extend the benefits of reservation to

so-called Dalit Christians will also have the same harmful effect. The fact that the Congress and some other parties are disregarding even court orders in these issues makes the matter more serious. The government must not go ahead with religion-based reservations. The BJP, as a party, stands opposed to it tooth and nail.

Naxalism is partly a result of lopsided socio-economic development. On the one hand, the state made some investments in steel plants, railways and aviation. On the other hand, basic irrigation, health and connectivity to villages were systematically ignored. This has led to subsequent generations of our rural population thronging to urban areas. As a result, the ratio of our urban-rural population today stands at approximately 28:72.

The indiscriminate expansion of urban population has led to slums thriving in every city. This has imposed an acute burden on urban infrastructure which, in several cities, is on the brink of total collapse. Other than that, it has aggravated the divide between 'haves' and 'have-nots', leading to abject frustration in a large chunk of our population. The less resolute among this chunk are often tempted to the world of crime as a 'perceived' means to bridge the gap. In many rural and tribal areas of the country, this frustration has already assumed a violent form.

Naxalism, the second major threat today to India's internal security and, indeed, to our democratic system itself, must be countered with a firm hand. Both, the theory and practice of Maoism, are completely alien to everything that India holds in high esteem. Let us not forget that foreign forces are actively fomenting unrest in India and encouraging Maoists to exploit the situation. I will urge the government to show absolutely no leniency towards Maoist leaders. Sadly, even after the ghastly Naxal attack in Chhattisgarh on 25 May 2013, which killed 30 people, including the veteran Congress leader, VC Shukla, the

Central government does not feel the need to review it's strategy in fighting the Naxal menace.

The patronage enjoyed by these groups from so-called civil rights activists is equally dangerous. I will advise Naxal sympathisers not to dress up this murderous ideology in clothes of legitimacy. Of course, all-out efforts should be made to accelerate pro-poor and corruption-free development in areas affected by Naxal violence. I have, personally, always advocated drawing up new schemes for tribal welfare. In fact, there is tremendous scope to generate employment opportunities for tribals in the biofuel sector as well as the bamboo industry. As a party, the BJP is committed to reaching out to the most underprivileged sections of society. However, under no circumstances can we allow anybody to take the law into their own hands.

A section of supposed intellectuals, that has a soft corner for Maoists, has endlessly tried to project the Naxal menace as a political problem and not as a law and order problem. They are free to view it whichever way they like. But when Naxals kill our security professionals at will, the government cannot sit as a silent spectator. Government inaction on the issue has only encouraged the Naxals to carry out their exploits with greater fearlessness.

THE NORTH-EAST

The situation in the North-East is another cause of concern for us, particularly the current scenario in Assam. The state government continues to develop cold feet while dealing with terrorist and secessionist elements, as also with the Bangladeshi infiltrators.

In the case of Assam, after the Assam Accord was signed in 1985 between the Centre, the state and the All Assam Students Union (AASU) with its thrust on detection, deletion (from the voters' list) and deportation of illegal migrants, a deadline of 31 March 2010 was set for updating the National Register of

Citizens (NRC). This so-called updating was an eyewash as the fact remains that the original NRC itself is not in proper order. We believe that a new NRC is the need of the hour. How long will the Congress-led governments at the Centre and the state wait before Assam witnesses the creation of a region of foreign nationals within its own boundaries?

The Centre's complete denial of the infiltration problem from Bangladesh, and even tacit support to it, was bound to create unrest among the local populace. And so it was. Violent clashes between Bodo tribals and Bangladeshi infiltrators, which broke out in July 2012, claimed over 50 lives besides rendering over 400,000 people homeless. What is shocking is that our Prime Minister, who has been a Rajya Sabha member from Assam for the past twenty-two years, has never acknowledged this problem, let alone talk about it. Even though the violence has been controlled, the situation continues to remain grim and, should the Centre not initiate immediate steps to address the infiltration problem, similar clashes are bound to recur in the future.

Manipur also continues to be in the grip of militant (or insurgent) groups. Here, the government machinery is completely paralysed and public life is continuously allowed to be held hostage by the underground terrorists. In so far as creating infrastructure for development in this region is concerned, the government has done precious little even after the creation of the Ministry of Development of North-East Region in 2001.

When I see the unrest and conflict in society—whether it is due to some identity issue or issues like growing number of the poor, rising unemployment, starvation and unabated suicides of farmers—I ask myself: 'What is at the root of these problems?' The two conclusions that I have come to are: Firstly, all these problems are rooted in the wrong economic policies and bad governance that have plagued our country since Independence.

Secondly, the solutions to these problems cannot be found in a piecemeal manner to satisfy this or that section of society.

CORRUPTION

Having talked about the internal and external security challenges facing us today, I wish to dwell upon a scourge that has the potential to undo all of our achievements of the last several decades, if left unchecked—the menace of corruption.

According to the Comptroller and Auditor General's (CAG) report, the total loss incurred by the Government of India due to the 2G scam (in rolling out second generation telecommunication in the country in 2008-09) is approximately ₹176,000 crore. As far as the 2010 Commonwealth Games fraud is concerned, newer cases of financial misappropriations keep surfacing every now and then, which makes it difficult to confirm the exact scale of losses.

Next in line was the Coal Allocation Scam or Coalgate. In a draft report issued in March 2012, the Comptroller and Auditor General of India (CAG) accused the government of allocating coal blocks in an inefficient manner during 2004-2009. The CAG final report, subsequently tabled in Parliament, put the loss figure at ₹185,591 crore.

The UPA government has also shown no interest in bringing back black money from India stacked in Swiss banks. A humungous sum of money of the Indian people has been stashed away in these foreign banks. I am surprised that the government, in all these years, has failed to draw up a plan of action that would ensure that such illegal money, which is deposited in various parts of the world, is brought to our country and deposited into our government treasury. In 2010, the Supreme Court has questioned our government's reluctance on the matter. It had directed the Solicitor General of India to seek instructions from the Centre to disclose the names of secret account holders who have deposited huge amounts of illegal money, estimated to be in lakhs of crores of rupees, in foreign banks. Sadly, nothing of the sort has happened since. What is worse is that the White Paper on Black Money, presented by our former Finance Minister, Pranab Mukherjee (who is now the esteemed President of the country), on 21 May 2012, turned out to be an exercise in futility. Its inability to fix a number to the size of the black economy from India rendered the whole exercise meaningless.

Such gross indifference towards corruption is a huge roadblock in the country's progress and well-being. It is like someone continuously robbing your house or bank lockers, and you are sitting like a mute spectator. It goes without saying that our supposedly honest Prime Minister, Manmohan Singh, has taken very few steps to check dishonesty. At one point, he even blamed the 'compulsions of coalition politics' for the numerous scams.

May I ask then, has the Congress consciously decided to outsource corruption to its coalition partners as a mantra for the government's survival?

Let us understand that the mass movement against corruption (July-August 2011), led by social activist Anna Hazare, is not something that happened overnight. People had been feeling increasingly helpless and taken for a ride by the UPA government. I feel sad that in such despondent times, people often tend to paint all politicians as 'corrupt', which is not true.

As for fighting terrorism, fighting corruption also requires political will, which the UPA government lacks. The BJP, on the other hand, has always shown greater will to fight this scourge.

One of the main causes of our concern has been the funding of elections. Unworthy candidates often pump in illegal money to buy votes, leading to an unholy nexus between politicians and criminals. I wish to inform my readers that the BJP was the first party to set up a corpus fund, called the *Aajeevan Sahyog Nidhi* for the purpose of reserving funds for election campaigns. This fund, which was established way back in 1993, is formed by small yearly contributions by a large number of party well-wishers. The BJP is the only party to have instituted this kind of a clean-funding mechanism.

When the NDA government was in power, we also introduced several electoral reforms to tackle corruption in politics. By the Ninety-first Amendment to the Constitution, introduced in 2003, the number of cabinet berths was limited to just 15 per cent of the total number of members of the House of People. The NDA government introduced a key amendment to omit Paragraph Three of the Tenth Schedule. This particular paragraph spelt out exemptions from disqualifications in the event of splits constituting one-third of the strength of the parent party. The reason for carrying out this change was that the paragraph allowed wholesale defections, while individual defections were considered illegal according to the rest of the Schedule. By the omission of Paragraph Three, the presiding officers of state legislatures and Parliament were left with very little discretion and scope for its abuse. This move also ensured that the decision of the Parliament and state legislatures would be entirely based on the facts of individual cases.

Again, during the rule of the NDA, in April 2003, a Representation of the People (Amendment) Bill was passed by the Parliament to replace the secret ballot system with an open ballot in the elections to the Rajya Sabha.

The Elections and Other Related Laws (Amendment) Bill 2003, which aimed at eliminating the influence of money power and black money support in elections to the Parliament and state assemblies, was passed for this purpose. The Representation of the People Act 1951 was suitably amended to allow companies, subject to the Companies Act, to make donations to political parties.

Unfortunately, in the nine years that the UPA has been in power, it has not followed up on the initiatives taken by us. Its gross mismanagement of the Lokpal Bill and its consequences are only too well known to need elaboration. We must remember that ours is a nation of immense diversities. Every section of our society has legitimate aspirations. But the fulfillment of these aspirations has to be a part of a holistic approach, guided by what is good for the nation as a whole. Harmony and balance are the cornerstones of the architecture of every creation of Mother Nature. Why shouldn't the same be true of human society? The harmonious development of individuals and society was the hallmark of Pandit Upadhyaya's treatise of 'Integral Humanism', which the BJP regards as its guiding philosophy. This is, today, nowhere to be seen in the scheme of things of policymakers in our country.

The Congress party's policies have resulted in severe imbalances in the country's development. These inequalities are both social and geographical in nature. In our march towards economic prosperity, often our people are encouraged to violate norms and regulations, with the rich and the powerful leading the way. This has a harmful impact on the moral, social and cultural fabric of India. The first and foremost task in correcting India's development imbalance is to follow the principle of *Antyodaya*. The eradication of abject poverty and providing basic necessities to every individual in society should be the goal of the Central and state governments. Long before I entered politics, I was moved by the following lines from Sant Tukaram, a prominent saint and spiritual poet of the Bhakti movement in India. I continue to seek inspiration from these lines even today.

> *Je kaa ranjale gaanjele, tyaasi mhane jo aapule!*
> *Tochi saadhu olakhaava, Dev tethechi jaanaava!*
> (One who embraces the disadvantaged and the oppressed, the downtrodden and the suffering as his own, is a true sadhu or a pious person. God dwells in his/her abode.)

Since the BJP is the main opposition party at the Centre, it is our duty to oppose and resist the wrong policies of the government. We shall perform this role resolutely.

People, however, expect more from us. As a party that has governed at the Centre, and that aspires to do so again, it is also our duty to evolve practical solutions to the multifarious problems that India has been facing.

Neither the people, nor we are happy with India's socio-economic development, which is full of imbalances and governance deficit, corruption and inefficiency.

As I have said earlier, most problems before the nation have very little to do with caste, creed, language or other such factors. They are rooted in the wrong policies of development and wrong kind of governance. I must point out here that today, the nation has an energy shortfall of 70,232 MU and we have no stocks of coal for power generation under the Twelfth Plan. This energy deficit is making this great nation development-starved, thanks mainly to the absolute lack of foresight.

The BJP, as a party, is proud of the initiatives and achievements of the NDA government. Now, based on our experience of governance at the Centre and in the states, we should conceptualise, propagate and implement an alternative model of development and governance.

I regard this to be one of the most important tasks before the party.

I had just one guiding thought in my mind from the moment I was given the job of party chief and this thought continues to inspire me: That I will propagate the politics of addition and not subtraction. What I mean by that is simple. We need to reach out to more and more sections of society. We need to increase our vote share by 10 per cent if we have to come to power again. That can only happen if our approach is constructive. Therein lies the need to chart out a new course for the individual and the party.

Everything can be explained to the people, on the single condition that you want them to understand.

—Frantz Fanon

THREE

Engine of Growth

The Mistakes

The conception or the start of a journey is often the most important determinant of the shape that journey will eventually take. Thus, the economic policies that we, as a country, adopted as an independent nation, cast a heavy bearing on the nature and rate of our country's growth over the next several decades.

As I begin my journey of communicating with you, I too face a difficult choice: Where do I start from? There is, after all, no dearth of development issues to talk about.

My choice is finally based on two important factors. The broad economic policies of the country are critical to the health of a nation. While we may have erred in adopting certain incorrect policies in the early years, how does one explain the government's complete helplessness today? While the GDP growth rate reached 7.8 per cent in March 2011, the exorbitant inflation rate also went up to 9.30 per cent in 2012. This nullifies all our gains. What baffles the people of our country even more is that our government, led by an 'economist Prime Minister' has remained clueless and indifferent throughout, letting the situation go from bad to worse.

When we delve into our economy, there are several questions that are bound to crop up. One wonders if we were two decades too late in opening up our economy. Two decades is a long time in the life of a nation. Had we taken the decisions we took in 1991 in say, 1971, the GDP growth rate that we have achieved today could possibly have been obtained in 1991. In that case, it might well have been possible for us to march ahead of our neighbour, China.

There is another important aspect that demands an answer: Why did successive governments consistently neglect agriculture and villages when Mahatma Gandhi's basic idea of a progressive nation had its roots in self-equipped villages?

The answers to these two questions are a saga of squandered opportunities, which I have delved into later, on my take on Nehruvian Socialism.

Coming to the present, the last few years haven't been the best years from an economic perspective. India's consistently sliding growth rate, burgeoning current account deficit and the free fall of the rupee have led to panic in the financial markets and driven away potential investors. This grim situation, thus, necessitates a thorough introspection and discussion on various aspects of the nation's economic policy.

As a member of a political party, I too subscribe to a certain ideology. That ideology supports a certain line of thinking on economic issues and I am committed to that thinking.

What should be our line of thought and resultant plan of action if we are to find a solution to the crisis of overall economic slowdown? The onus for devising the right economic policy rests upon the Central government. However, state governments also have a role to play in finding out the solution so that workers, farmers and other wage earners are saved from the adverse effects of recession.

When India got freedom from British rule and Pandit Jawaharlal Nehru became the Prime Minister, he adopted the Soviet model of Socialist economy for the country as he was influenced by it. At that time, it was decided to keep all the sectors under government control. The defense sector, anyway, has always been under government control due to the high level of confidentiality required in its operations.

Pandit Nehru was a visionary in his own right, which reflected in the decisions he took. On the other hand, I tend to agree more with the thoughts of Pandit Upadhyaya and Dr Mookerjee.

I have travelled across some thirty-five countries, which includes travelling extensively in the USA and Israel. From my observations of the economic policies of so many different countries, I can say this as a universal truth: The economic policy of any country cannot be decided solely upon the thoughts and views written in books. If a book describes an animal as an elephant, we need not accept it to be so without being personally convinced that the said animal is not a bull. We need to take decisions based on practical applicability of theoretical knowledge.

Pandit Nehru invested heavily in iron and steel plants. Similarly, he built dams and bridges, as they were very important. His government established several power plants in the country as well. After Independence, until 2006, the Government of India had invested more than ₹560,000 crore in the public sector, a majority of them dead investments.

It is worth going back in time and examining if we took

the right economic decisions post-Independence. What ought to have been the key areas of focus for us?

To simplify things, we can divide the entire development agenda into two broad heads—agriculture and industries. For industrial progress, four basic necessities ought to be taken care of: Water, electricity, connectivity and communications. Similarly, for progress in the field of agriculture, the things necessary are: Water, irrigation, better seeds and, most importantly, facilitating those small-scale industries that process agricultural by-products.

RURAL DEVELOPMENT

As a nation, we have not taken care of these crucial requirements. When the NDA government was in power at the Centre, Vajpayeeji had launched the Pradhan Mantri Gram Sadak Yojana 2000. Out of 825,000 villages in India, there were no roads in approximately 330,000 villages. Rural development, until then, had not been given the priority it deserved.

Massive investments were made, instead, in steel plants and India Tourism Development Corporation (ITDC) hotels. Consequently, a majority of these investments proved to be dead investments. Sometime ago, Bharat Heavy Electricals Limited (BHEL), which is a Government of India undertaking, involved in the production of turbine and boilers, had orders for three years but they could not fulfil them. Instead, various Indian organisations handed over their orders to the Shanghai Electric Company based in China. This company has the capacity to manufacture electrical equipment that can produce 60,000 MW of electricity every year. The cost of these orders was approximately ₹110,000 crore. In other words, if we say that we are running the Chinese economy, it may not be a matter of surprise. One question often clouds my mind: Since BHEL has a technological collaboration with Siemens, why didn't they expand this company to meet their requirements? Why are the orders of our nation being doled out so generously to China?

I guess it has to do with the clumsy operating style of government undertakings. Being a public sector company, BHEL is controlled by ministers. Each proposal is put forward in the cabinet for its approval. Often, there is no comment or discussion for several months. As a result, they do not come to any conclusion. It is a sad fact that we have made no attempts to expand the facilities we already have, power generation projects being the worst sufferers in the process.

When I was the PWD minister in Maharashtra, we had extensive debates on various models of private sector participation. In 1996, when I visualised the flyovers project for Mumbai with a system of toll revenues, I faced criticism from all quarters, including my own party. A well-wisher asked me, 'What is the use of constructing the bridge by collecting the "toll" money? Why do we need to collect money from people in order to build the flyovers?'

I built flyovers with the help of money earned from the capital market and used the budget allocated to PWD for building metalled roads in 16,000 villages. In Gadchiroli district of Maharashtra, which has a large population of tribals and has often witnessed instances of Maoist violence, I ensured huge public investment in road construction. My priority has always been to reach out to the poorest of the poor. In areas with higher per capita income, I feel people should be ready to pay a bit extra for improved services. This, in my opinion, is the most feasible way in which disparities across various sections of society can be bridged.

Thus, the entire amount of government finance, in my tenure, was made available for poor people. The idea behind this was to give topmost priority to the most backward districts.

The resources of the government must reach the unprivileged. In rural areas, especially in Gadchiroli, things still have not improved much. Several rural areas, even today, experience power load-shedding that goes up to eighteen hours every day. Lack of human resources and physical infrastructure has hit the education system in these areas. Schools exist but there are no school buildings. Where school building and teachers are present, there are no students. Where all three are available, there is no quality education. The condition of life in some of our backward regions is such that there is a dearth of medical expertise, leaving a majority of hospitals doctor-less. In case doctors get transferred to a place like the Gadchiroli district, they take the help of ministers and get their transfers revoked.

Most of the problems of rural India are the result of a lack of attention. Gandhiji had truly said, 'We want maximum production with the involvement of maximum number of persons.' In our country, we ought to have ideally striven to obtain the maximum production possible by involving more and more people. However, Jawaharlal Nehru's formula was different: He appears to have wanted maximum production with the help of technology. Both these thoughts have their own importance. But, in the process, we have, somewhere, ignored Gandhiji's vision.

AGRICULTURE

There are some institutions in the country which manufacture bamboo-related products and employ tribals in this exercise. In the Bhandara district of Maharashtra, tribals are engaged in manufacturing various products from bamboo stalks. For instance, bamboo mats made by them are used in the western coal fields, fetching revenue worth crores of rupees. Thus, the jungles of our country can provide employment opportunities in bamboo-related business to at least 2-2.5 million people, if we have a plan of action. At present, however, the bamboo business is on the verge of decline and workers are losing employment. One of the reasons for this decline has been the misconceptions surrounding 'westernisation and modernisation'.

We should oppose westernisation, but promote modernisation. Today, technology is indispensable and if our farmers do not keep pace with the latest advances in technology then our agricultural productivity will continue to remain low. With this view in mind, I promoted a concept called Agrovision, which is an exhibition where the best agricultural products and the most innovative methods of farming are showcased for the benefit of farmers all across the country. Agrovision's core theme is to build sustainable livelihoods and increase farmers' incomes. The four-day Agrovision 2012, held at Reshimbagh ground in Nagpur, concluded with an overwhelming response, with over 350,000 people visiting the national expo showcasing agro-related products and services from 150 organisations. Over 60,000 farmers participated in 36 workshops and 20 experts deliberated possibilities of promoting bio energy. In May 2012, I led a delegation of 50 farmers from the Vidarbha region to the 18th International Agricultural Technology Exhibition, Agritech in Israel, with a view to explore new technologies and practices to empower the Indian farming community and promote a more progressive and sustainable rural economy. We participated in a series of conferences and meetings with a focus on agro-technologies, water management, including water treatment technologies, maritime transportation development and irrigation technologies.

While on the one hand, I am happy to note that a small section of our farmers is ready to embrace the latest agricultural technologies, it is also quite disturbing to find that a large number of our farmers do not have access to basic irrigation facilities.

Among all the other sectors, in my opinion, agriculture is the most crucial sector in our country's economy. However, it has not been given due importance. Irrigation in our country is a 'state' subject, though there is a ministry in the Central government for water resources. Considering that the supply of adequate water alone increases the productivity of an agricultural holding by two and a half times, its overbearing impact on the quality of life is only too well known.

Once I was travelling from Satara and Sangli towards Solapur in the interiors of Maharashtra, when a thought struck me. We were passing through a village and I told the government official who was accompanying me, 'This village gets proper supply of water. Tell me if I'm wrong.' My guess was correct. The official was surprised and asked me, 'Western Maharashtra is largely a dry region, how could you say water is available in this village without having been here?'

I told him that the village that has access to water, invariably houses cemented shops, the eateries are crowded, while the shops buzz with customers. In other words, greater positive activity is visible in such villages. On the other hand, in the village where water is scarce, one can spot old carts made of tin, empty shops and sad-looking people. Villages do not develop unless and until they get adequate supply of water.

The current situation is quite bleak, though. No doubt, some investments have taken place lately in irrigation and road projects but that again is only 40 per cent of what it ought to be. There are regions in the country which are parched, forcing people either to commit suicide or to move out of these areas. According to the information I have, approximately ₹80,000 crore worth of irrigation projects in Maharashtra are on hold. The production cost is increasing rapidly. The estimated cost of the Gosikhurd Irrigation Project in the Vidarbha region of

Maharashtra was ₹461 crore way back in 1995. Today, the cost of the project has increased by about eighteen times because of inordinate delays.[1]

RURAL INDUSTRY

Another major concern is the escalated prices of raw materials like cement, which in turn has increased the cost of construction of houses and other necessary infrastructure, adversely impacting the quality of life. This is where the government needs to show more foresight.

Thus, in all construction projects, I strongly recommend mixing 30 per cent fly-ash into cement to make it stronger. Much of the concerns about fly-ash being harmful to the environment have remained unsubstantiated. Instead, fly-ash is much sought after today for most construction work. This is the power of innovation. Fly-ash from Nasik has been used for construction of the airports at Doha and Dubai. The cost of one 50 kg bag of cement is approximately ₹300. Without taxes, this bag will cost only about ₹70. Even with all the taxes, the cost will go up to ₹112 only. Yet, a bag of cement is today sold for ₹310. Mixing fly-ash with cement will bring down the cost of several projects by reducing the total quantity of cement that is used.

The government should come forward and provide incentives to all businessmen who intend to set up cement plants. The government should, in fact, try to work out collaborations with private industrialists, whereby it could hold 35 per cent stake in the new cement plants and have the rights to over 35 per cent of the total cement produced by these plants. The government can use these resources for different purposes. This cement should be made available to the government after adding 15 per cent as manufacturing tax. If cement is made available at this rate, then there will be a direct 15 per cent reduction in the total cost of irrigation and road construction projects, where this cement may be used.

Our vast spending on the import of crude oil is another area of concern. India's annual spending on import of crude oil in 2011-12 was in excess of ₹995,000 crore. Needless to say, this expenditure exerts a huge pressure on our economy.

Thus, it calls for some amount of far-sightedness to link this problem with the problem of unemployment prevalent in our rural sector and see if we can come out with a comprehensive plan that addresses both issues. Vajpayeeji had a vision for this: Diversification of agriculture towards energy and power sector. Increased biofuel usage can do wonders for our economy by reducing our expenditure on import of crude oil. It will also provide another source of income to the farmers in our country, besides helping the environment. I will be talking about this in more detail when I share my views on unconventional sources of energy.

Energy deficit is another major handicap which holds us back as a nation. We must explore alternative ways of electricity generation so that the problem of load-shedding is solved and people get employment. Similarly, we need to be more innovative with our farming techniques. In America, sugar is manufactured out of maize. In Europe, sugar is manufactured from beetroot, while we are still manufacturing sugar out of sugarcane.

The last few decades have witnessed a vast migration from rural to urban areas. If villagers get employment opportunities and adequate infrastructure—metalled roads, schools, potable water, healthy milk-producing animals—in their village, why then would they migrate to a city just to take up odd jobs as a peon or a servant?

PRIVATISATION

I wish to emphasise that, to optimise its economic progress, a nation needs to provide a level playing field to its private entrepreneurs. The government's job is not to do business. Instead, it is the government's responsibility to formulate and set in motion the right regulations that would aid private industrial houses, and ensure and protect the interests of consumers.

Economic liberalisation has brought huge gains to the private sector. More importantly, it has resulted in a qualitative improvement in services to the end user.

The telecom sector is a live example of this improvement. When we did not have a phone, I would think several times before calling up my sister who lived in a neighbouring town, as even a one minute conversation would cost more than ₹50. Today, I have to pay less than ₹1 per call.

Who has benefitted the most from this?

It is a myth that technology benefits only the rich. On the contrary, the biggest beneficiaries of the telecom growth have been the poor. Today, a vegetable seller talks on the phone and finds out the rate of tomatoes in other markets. Similarly, fishermen get weather updates on their cell phone. In fact, KPMG analysts carried out a study in September 2010 which suggested that Indian consumers, including illiterate sections, often embrace technology faster than those in more developed countries. Out of the number of people who were contacted for this study, 38 per cent said that they were using their phones for shopping and 43 per cent were carrying out banking transactions through the phone. These figures indicate every sign of the telecom sector growing further in the coming years.

This revolution did not take place overnight and we should be gracious in giving credit where it is due. We must salute Rajiv Gandhi and Sam Pitroda for setting us up on the path of technology. Pramod Mahajan, who was the Minister for Telecommunications in the NDA government between 2001-03, had further revolutionised communications in our country. Sadly today, the telecom sector is in the news for all the wrong reasons, with the country still coming to terms with the UPA government's 2G scam.

A similar revolution was seen in the aviation sector too. At first, Indian Airlines was the only company plying in the country. Now, there are several airlines. As a result, services have expanded and improved while flight prices have come down. This has obviously increased competition and companies have realised that competitive pricing is a must for their survival. As a result, passengers have benefitted enormously. The archaic principle of equality does not approve of liberalisation but liberalisation and privatisation should happen. There is no other alternative. Nobody can stop it.

Let us consider the present-day scenario in China. The bulk of the investment in the country has been done by the Chinese living in the USA, Indonesia, Malaysia and Singapore. The Chinese settled in America are very rich. As China has an open economy, the non-resident Chinese have invested significantly in all major sectors in their country. These investments have played a big role in catapulting China to the position of the economic superpower which it is today.

We need not get disappointed by our present inadequacies, however. In the eighteenth century, we were ruled by the Mughals. In the nineteenth century, the Union Jack replaced them. America was the superpower of the twentieth century. The twenty-first century is the age of information technology. Every year, the Indian economy gets about ₹120,000 crore worth of capital, routed via this industry. Indian software engineers have flagged themselves in the entire world. The skills they possess are among the best. However, we need to do more to make the best technological education available to the poorer sections of society. We need to provide more incentives like free land, subsidised electricity and other facilities so that more engineering and medical colleges are set up. This step can ensure that the cost of education comes down. The biggest beneficiary of competition is always the poor.

I have an earnest appeal to the government: We need to have a clear plan of action about what we need to do in the field of education, agriculture, industry, infrastructure, energy, etc. Let us finalise a concrete plan of action in this direction.

There are many people in politics, especially in India, who convert opportunities into problems.

While deciding upon future policies, we need to also give due importance to devising policies that will empower newer concepts of growth. The benefits of progress must reach the poorest of the poor.

A time has come when we need to set aside books on economy and instead devise economic policies, based on our practical understanding of the challenges emerging in the twenty-first century. The need of the hour is not necessarily an economist prime minister but leaders who apply common sense and practical approach towards the country's economic concerns. That is what the present situation demands and that is what will benefit people the most.

The people of this country have evolved a lot in the last two decades. They are least interested in political rivalry or one-upmanship between two rival political parties. Today, more than anything else, they want employment. Their main concern is development. The time has come when we need to usher in 'progressive politics' or the 'politics of development' in our country.

WHAT AILED NEHRUVIAN SOCIALISM?

Before I dwell upon the economic or industrial policy of our first government headed by Nehru in detail, let me travel a few hundred years back into our history. This is important to understand the kind of stakes that were involved in our economic policy post-Independence.

The Indian subcontinent ranks high among the world's most-invaded lands. There were two primary reasons for these invasions. One, the Indus Valley civilisation was an immensely fragmented one, with a multitude of kingdoms that had little sense of unity. But the more important reason was the massive advancement made by the civilisation in various spheres.

In the fourth century AD, King Chandragupta II united all of northern India into a great empire which explains why the Gupta period is described as the golden age of Indian history. Under their rule, the arts, including poetry and literature, flourished. The exquisite Ajanta and Ellora caves were fashioned in this period. The Gupta period extended from 320 AD to 540 AD. But around 480 AD, the Huns invaded India from the north and destroyed the Gupta Empire.

The country subsequently broke into multiple kingdoms again, which were then invaded by the Turks, the Mughals and the British. In 1947, when we emerged as an independent nation after centuries of imposed foreign rule, we had a magnificent opportunity to revive the golden age of the Gupta period.

The key driver for such a revival would have needed to be the state's economic policy. Nehru had two options in front of him: One was the Gandhian philosophy of making India a republic of self-sufficient villages, employing indigenous methods, materials and talent. The other was to expedite technological advancement through investment in heavy industries, particularly steel. Nehru, who was very impressed by the Socialist Soviet model of development, chose the second, despite the fact that the majority of our people lived in villages at that time.

The means adopted to usher in this revolution were more damaging. Given his Socialist mindset, foreign investment was ruled out; so was the involvement of Indian private industrial houses. Our government, thus, approached the Soviet Union and Germany to help us set up steel plants with foreign aid.

Worse, the Industrial Policy Resolution of 1956 reserved seventeen industries exclusively for the public sector. These included iron and steel, mining and heavy electrical plants. Although the door was not explicitly closed on the private sector, the constraints imposed by the licensing system led to a monopolistic and centralised system which impeded growth in every conceivable way.

The centralised Socialist-democratic economy had many drawbacks: It wiped out competition and led to reduced productivity; it killed entrepreneurship; it drained our economy; worse, it led to a corrupt and inefficient bureaucracy. The whole concept of the state doubling up as entrepreneur had its limitations, more so in a country like ours where the size of the population was way bigger than what all of the state's efforts could cater to. The results were not unexpected. As decades went by, we continued to battle an acute deficit of multiple kinds, which failed all our poverty alleviation initiatives.

Had a simultaneous process of integrated, rural and agricultural development been pursued with Nehru's 'Socialist industrial development', the results might have been different. Agriculture, instead, constantly suffered from neglect and a step-motherly treatment. To my understanding, our biggest fallacy was to make irrigation a state subject. Our Constitution lays down the legislative and functional jurisdiction of the Union, state and local governments regarding 'water'. Under the scheme of the Constitution, **'water' is basically a state subject. The Union intervenes only in the case of a dispute between states regarding**

sharing of river water. Given how critically agriculture is dependent upon irrigation, this was a colossal blunder.

It will be interesting to note what some of the more successful economies of the world did in the period between 1947 to 1991.

In South Korea, the government provided cheap credit to private entrepreneurs when it did not have the resources to invest in strategic industries. Japan employed competition as a tool to fuel and precipitate growth. In the 1970s, Malaysia began to imitate the four Asian Tiger economies—the Republic of Korea (South Korea), the Republic of China (Taiwan), the then British Crown Colony of Hong Kong and the Republic of Singapore. Malaysia committed itself to a transition from being reliant on mining and agriculture to an economy that depends more on manufacturing, thereby adopting a multi-sector economic model. Singapore, on the other hand, showed great courage in whole-heartedly opening up its markets.

It was only in 1991 that a do-or-die situation made the Indian government change its rules. The country faced a serious economic crisis then. The government was close to default, its central bank had refused new credit and foreign exchange reserves had reduced to the point that India could barely finance three weeks' worth of imports and wages.

Credit must go where it is due. And I whole-heartedly appreciate PV Narasimha Rao, who despite running a minority government, showed the courage and enterprise which other Congress prime ministers lacked.

The Government of India headed by Rao, between 1991-96, decided to usher in several reforms that are collectively termed as 'liberalisation'. The maximum progress made by these reforms were in the areas of opening up to foreign investment, reforming capital markets, deregulating domestic business and reforming the trade regime. Liberalisation has done away with the licence raj (investment, industrial and import licensing) and ended many public sector monopolies, allowing automatic approval of Foreign Direct Investment (FDI) in many sectors.

Two decades later, the Indian economy has grown significantly. From 2004 until 2010, India's average quarterly GDP growth was 8.37 per cent, reaching a historical high of 10.10 per cent in September 2006, and a record low of 5.50 per cent in December 2004.

If we go solely by these figures, only a fool can dispute the growth of the Indian economy. But, as they say, statistics often conceals more than what it reveals.

There is another side to the coin—33 per cent of our population earns less than ₹70 a day—and this only reinforces our greater fears: That the benefits of open markets have reached a small segment of our population and have only escalated the divide between the rich and the poor. Moreover, the steep inflation rates have led to overall rise in prices that has made the lives of the poor even more miserable.

INCREASE IN POVERTY

The failure of the Congress policies has been affirmed by official sources themselves. A committee, headed by the prime minister's economic advisor, Suresh Tendulkar (in a December 2009 report), has revealed that the number of poor in India has increased by 10 per cent. The report said that poverty in rural India stands at 42 per cent. Contrast this with the stark fact that, in recent years, the wealth of a small section of India's rich has increased astronomically. Is this not a warning signal that a policy review is needed? According to this committee's finding, around 410 million people in India live under the estimated poverty line set by the UN at USD 1.25 a day—100 million more than all previous estimates. The conditions of the poor in certain parts of the country are believed to be even worse than those in sub-Saharan Africa. India is said to account for one-third of the world's poor, with earnings of less than USD 2 a day. Even though the GDP growth of the nation stands at 6.1 per cent, (as in December 2012), only about 1 per cent of the total GDP is directed towards expenditure on healthcare.[2]

A similar disclosure has come from the United Nations Department of Economic and Social Affairs (UNDESA), whose data punctures holes in the UPA government's tall claims about their achievements. UNDESA data has revealed that, in 2009 alone, 13.6 million more people became poor. This shows that the Congress-led government, far from achieving the goal of '*Garibi Hatao*', has actually succeeded in '*Garibi Badhao*'. In this context, I also recollect a report which was presented by economist Arjun Sengupta to the Prime Minister of India in 2006. As the chairman of the National Commission for Enterprises in Unorganised Sector (NCEUS), he had pointed out in the report that 77 per cent of our population does not live on more than ₹20 per day. There cannot be a more telling commentary on the failure of our economy.

As such, today, the need to urgently devise a comprehensive policy for agricultural growth has become more critical than ever before. It will be interesting to note here that, even in the time of Pandit Nehru, American economists had advised India to invest and focus on agriculture. These suggestions were treated with scepticism then, just as most other advice from the US. It is ironical that four decades later, in the changed global scenario, India finds itself closer to the US than ever before. There is a vast scope for the two countries to collaborate on the agricultural front.

There is an urgent need for course correction.

Indispensability of Public Private Partnership

Ancient India was well known as a trading hub. Indians were known for their entrepreneurial skills and there is evidence to suggest that they had been engaged in trade with Central Asia and Europe, as early as in the first century. The Romans provide us the first written account of their trading relations with India. Roman chronicler and historian Pliny recorded: 'Not a year passed in which India did not take fifty million sesterces away from Rome.'

In 1600 AD, the East India Company was formed in Britain for the specific purpose of pursuing trade with India and China. There are many other instances which vouch for India's supremacy in trade and entrepreneurship in the earlier centuries.

After Independence, our 'protectionist' policies inflicted great damage to this spirit of Indian entrepreneurship. When I opted for the PPP model in 1997, one of the key factors that influenced my choice was my faith in Indian entrepreneurs. By suppressing private entrepreneurship initiatives in heavy investment areas, we had impeded the pace of infrastructural development in the country.

I was glad that I was proved right. The time frame in which the Mumbai-Pune Expressway was completed and the quality of the work done, bear testimony to this. Fifteen years after I adopted the PPP model, today, I am equally happy to see the acceptance that it has received in India as the most feasible way of accelerating the infrastructural growth in our country.

It is important for us to understand here why this model is such an indispensable tool for all developing economies.

Public private partnership describes a government service or private business venture, which is funded and operated through a partnership of government and one or more private sector companies. Therefore, the partnership involves a contract between a public sector authority and a private party, in which the latter provides a public service and assumes substantial financial, technical and operational risk in the project. In some types of partnership, the cost of using the service is borne exclusively by the users of the service and not by the taxpayer. In other types of PPP, notably the private finance initiative, capital investment is made by the private sector on the strength of a contract with government to provide agreed services, and the cost of providing the service is borne wholly or in part by the government. Government contributions to the model may also be in kind (notably, the transfer of existing assets). In projects that are aimed at creating public goods like in the infrastructure sector, the government may provide a capital subsidy in the form of a one-time grant, so as to make it more attractive to the private investors. In some other cases, the government may support the project by providing revenue subsidies, including tax breaks or by providing guaranteed annual revenues for a fixed period.

In the Indian context, the increase in PPP projects has been facilitated by several factors. Ever since the process of economic reforms started in 1991, the world began to see India as an investment-friendly destination. A stable democracy and independent democratic institutions only helped in this process.

The NDA government gave further impetus to this initiative by setting up the Ministry for Disinvestment in December 1999. This Ministry was meant to formulate a systematic policy approach to disinvestment and privatisation of Public Sector Units (PSUs). In 2004, the Ministry was dismantled and the same task was assigned to a new department, under the Ministry of Finance.

There are several reasons why partnership between public and private sectors is a must in today's world.

Private parties need to be made stakeholders in the

country's progress and development. If we suppress our entrepreneurs, they will be forced to look at investing in other countries. The present state of globalisation offers the Indian entrepreneur multiple opportunities even in the supposedly backward African countries. To make the best use of the skills of our entrepreneurs, we must be ready to provide them a sense of ownership in our key development projects.

As I have mentioned before, people tend to ignore this aspect completely but, in my opinion, the PPP model is also crucial from the point of view of improving the living conditions of the poorest of the poor. If all or most development projects in urban areas are executed through this model, then all government funds can be reserved for the most backward regions. This will help in ending the disparity between different regions and sections of society and will help in improving the social harmony in our country.

Over the years, the Indian economy has seen increased foreign investment, both through the equity markets (termed Foreign Institutional Investment or FII) and FDI. With her size and growth potential, India is considered an attractive market. Furthermore, a high Return on Investment (RoI) acts as another inducing factor that draws investors towards India.

The Eleventh Five Year Plan (2007-12) recognised the key role of infrastructure in accelerating the momentum of economic development. Accordingly, an investment of ₹2,056,150 crore was projected for the Eleventh Plan, which was more than twice the investment during the Tenth Plan. This ambitious target for investment in infrastructure was constrained by the limitations of budgetary allocations, especially in view of the renewed emphasis on social sectors. As a result, the role of private investment in funding infrastructure projects assumed greater significance in delivering the Eleventh Plan targets.

Available data suggests that about 34 per cent[4] of the total investment in infrastructure during the first two years of the Eleventh Five Year Plan came from private investment as compared to about 24.86 per cent during the Tenth Plan. The total investment in infrastructure during the Tenth Plan was ₹906,074 crore, of which ₹225,220 crore came from private investment. The projected private investment during the Eleventh Plan was ₹742,912 crore, which is about 82 per cent of the total investment made during the Tenth Plan.

I wish to take this discussion a step forward. As I have stated, PPP models have several variants. We can devise even more variants as long as it is a win-win situation for both the government and the private entity involved, and the partnership benefits the common man. The key is to explore innovative ways to exploit the PPP model and maximise our gains in the social sector.

Let us take the health sector for example. I have an idea which I would like to share here. If we were to provide free land and subsidised electricity to leading private sector healthcare providers to set up state-of-the-art hospitals in smaller towns or in needy areas and, in return, these hospitals would reserve 50 per cent of their wards and services for the poor and the underprivileged, not only would the poorest of the poor be provided treatment free of cost, but these hospitals could charge their normal rates from the remaining half.

Similarly, the PPP model can be exploited in the education sector. If we provide free land and electricity at minimal charges to the private sector to set up high-quality educational institutions in the rural areas and make it mandatory for them to reserve 50 per cent seats for the poor locals, it will bridge the gap between the rich and the poor. Moreover, there should be incentives for urban professionals to take up work in the rural areas.

Eventually, some years later, this experiment should lead to cross-migration and benefit the country as a whole.

Tourism is another sector whose potential remains untapped.

Kerala Tourism is an excellent example of the PPP model. The private sector in Kerala's tourism industry is way ahead of other states in marketing, service and operations. The Kerala Travel Mart, a buyer-seller biannual event, which takes place in Kochi, is run by the private sector. The state government plays a supporting role by encouraging the private partners to promote the state in the domestic and international market through road shows and tourism fairs. Another indicator of the active participation of private players here is the fact that 90 per cent of total houseboats in Kerala are owned by single or double-boat owners.

Tourism improves the economy of a place to a great extent. The local population is benefitted, directly or indirectly. Therefore, the tourism potential of all states must be tapped effectively. And the private sector has a pivotal role to play in this.

Our country has made remarkable progress since the license raj ended. The adoption and recognition of the viability of the PPP model has further precipitated progress. However, a lot more needs to be done. Optimising this model in the social sector is what will improve delivery of necessities like healthcare and quality education in the rural and under-developed regions of the country. This is what we must strive for with a sense of urgency.

Generosity is giving more than you can and pride is taking less than you need.

—Khalil Gibran

FOUR

Rural India

Farmer Suicides: Shocking Truth Behind the National Shame

When one talks about development, it is equally important to gain a proper understanding of issues that impede development. Farmers' suicide is a major problem in many parts of the country. An honest assessment of why the problem remains unabated will also provide some disturbing answers about what holds India back as a nation.

Farmers' suicide is not merely an issue that affects Vidarbha, Maharashtra or the country; today it is a matter of discussion all over the world. The ironical thing about these incidents in the Indian context is that the relief packages that were announced for the farmers have only aggravated the problem and increased the suicides.

There are two dimensions to the problem: One, the gross corruption and misappropriation of funds and relief packages meant for the poor farmers; two, the government's inaction on the critical issue of irrigation. It is shocking that while we keep debating the problem of farmers' suicides in every forum, no concrete steps have been taken to address either of these concerns. I will dwell upon both issues in detail.

In Vidarbha (east Maharashtra bordering Chhattisgarh and Andhra Pradesh), from the point of view of farming, three districts are important—Bhandara, Chandrapur, Gadchiroli—while half of the region of Nagpur is particularly important for the rice crop. On the other side, in western Vidarbha, soya bean and cotton are the major crops. If we talk about cotton, ever since the cotton monopoly purchase scheme was started, instead of benefitting the cotton producing farmers, there has been an increase in the number of suicides. Cotton is also produced in Gujarat in the Rajkot region. In Gujarat, on an average, the cotton yield for every acre of land is thrice that of the corresponding yield in the Vidarbha region.

To increase the production of cotton, if we decide to use chemical fertilisers and fountain irrigation system, then at the present per quintal rates of cotton, even the basic cost of investment will not be recovered. Similarly, the condition of soya bean producing farmers in the region has also worsened.

What is most saddening about the plight of Vidarbha is that there has never been a dearth of relief packages. However, a closer look reveals that all these packages either never took off or were grossly mismanaged.

RELIEF: A MYTH

In 2006, the Prime Minister announced a relief package worth ₹3,750 crore for 6 of the worst-affected districts of Vidarbha. It was subsequently decided that the farmers will get loans at 6 per cent interest. Have the farmers got the promised loans? The cooperative revolution in the region has also turned out to be a curse, instead of a blessing.

No loan was provided at 6 per cent interest. At many places, the loan provision has been stopped. Even where the loan was given, the farmers had to take it at 12-14 per cent interest. Farmers, who do not qualify for government loans, have to borrow from private moneylenders at exorbitant interest rates that range between 24-30 per cent. Besides, the banks themselves have become insolvent. Several banks have taken money, but nobody knows where this money is. That, anyway, is a separate story. Despite their mismanagement, the banks continue to enjoy the protection of the government.

After the Prime Minister's package, the Chief Minister of Maharashtra subsequently announced a package of ₹1,075 crore for the worst-affected districts of Vidarbha. What happened to that package? Will the government furnish an account of every penny distributed under this package? I challenge both the governments to bring out a White Paper on the fate of the money allotted under these packages. The people of this country ought to know the truth.

In Vidarbha, the 6 suicide-affected districts were provided ₹50 lakh each. Another ₹712 crore was set aside to do away with interest on loans. The beneficiaries of this largesse were the cooperative banks and not the farmers. The banks that were facing insolvency have now been revived due to these funds. Even as people are befooled by these packages, banks do big business.

There is a rule relating to cooperative bank loans to farmers: If a farmer has taken a loan of ₹10,000 and returned the entire amount, then he is not entitled to pay anything extra. However, cooperative banks have been regularly flouting these norms, with the result that taking a loan from these banks has become far more atrocious than obtaining the same from moneylenders. The government is a silent spectator to such malpractices.

Many of these cooperative banks are involved in huge scams—the Nanded District Bank is involved in a scam of ₹280 crore; Osmanabad District Bank, ₹285 crore; Nagpur District Bank, ₹150 crore and Wardha District Bank, ₹60 crore. These banks had been providing loans at an exorbitant rate of 14 per cent to the farmers: 5 per cent interest on the loan amount, 3 per cent commission for the state cooperative bank, 3 per cent commission for the district bank and 3 per cent commission for the Service Cooperative Society. Most of these cooperative banks in Maharashtra are run by influential leaders of the ruling Congress.

Surprisingly, in neighbouring Madhya Pradesh, which is a BJP-ruled state, the farmers are provided loan at a zero per cent interest rate. However, in Maharashtra, the government has become a puppet in the hands of bank owners and operators and in the process, has been exploiting the farmers. It is indeed an insult to the farming community of our country that, today, we can get the loan for a Mercedes car at the rate of 9 to 10 per cent, but if the farmers have to take loans for tractors, they need to pay 15 per cent interest. This, sadly, is a mockery of our claims to help the farmers.

I have evidence of misappropriation and loot of even cattle and fertilisers that were supposed to have been distributed among the farmers under the Prime Minister's package. Those responsible for this embezzlement enjoy the direct patronage of some of leaders in Maharashtra. I make this accusation with full responsibility as I have used the provisions of the Right to Information Act (RTI) to gather information on who all have benefitted from the relief packages. I have proof of politicians, including those who have been MLAs or MPs, acquiring cows from such packages. My information even suggests there could be a competition between leaders of the Congress and the Nationalist

Congress Party (NCP) on who is able to acquire more number of cows. It is indeed a national shame that these leaders must loot from the packages meant for impoverished farmers. No wonder then, that the relief packages remain a myth and the condition of farmers continues to deteriorate.

In his report released in 2007, the CAG had criticised the Maharashtra government for various irregularities in executing relief measures for Vidarbha's farmers. It is indeed sad that the relief packages meant to end farmers' suicides have actually aggravated the problem.

The other reason why the problem remains unabated is, of course, the miserably poor irrigation facilities available to the farmers in the region.

WATER, ROADS

As long as the villages are not developed, farmers will never progress. Till the time the per capita income of rural India does not increase, India's progress will not be balanced. There are four things which are very important for the progress of agriculture: One, the farmers must get the required amount of water; two, cheap electricity must be provided to them; three, good quality fertilisers and seeds must be made available to them; four, those industries that depend on the processing of agricultural by-products should be established in Special Economic Zones (SEZs). While we discuss SEZs in the context of big industrialists, we never think of establishing a textile industry under the SEZ scheme in the Yavatmal district for the benefit of cotton producing farmers.

There is a commonly prevalent habit of making excuses to cover up our failures. So, the fact that irrigation is not a 'Central' subject makes it easy for governments at the Centre to pass the onus on to the state governments. The state governments, in turn, always point to their limitations. However, where there is a strong will, finding a way is never impossible.

Just as irrigation, even construction of roads connecting villages is not on the Central list. In 2000, Prime Minister Vajpayeeji constituted a committee under my chairmanship, called the National Rural Road Development Committee. The core objective of this committee was to devise solutions to the problem of poor road connectivity in rural India. This committee also had the president of the National Bank for Agriculture and Rural Development (NABARD) and the Deputy Governor of the Reserve Bank of India (RBI) as its distinguished members. In my report, I advocated a pivotal role for the Central government in the planning and execution of roads connecting villages across the country. Based on my recommendations, an ambitious nationwide plan, called the Pradhan Mantri Gram Sadak Yojana, was launched by the Central government. The project, of course, had to battle its share of obstacles. At that point, the bureaucracy was up in arms against me, insisting that construction of village roads is the responsibility of the respective state governments and not the Central government.

Even then, I had told Vajpayeeji that due to unnecessary rules, hundreds of farmers starve in our villages, as their produce cannot reach cities. Due to the absence of roads, seriously ill people cannot be taken to hospitals. In 2000, even after 53 years of Independence, out of 825,000 villages in India, nearly 330,000 villages did not have all-weather roads. Thus, dismissing it as a 'subject' of the state government was not fair. The Central government ought to exercise its authority to change the rules that act as impediments in our progress, I had said. Vajpayeeji accepted my suggestion and, within ten days, he announced the Prime Minister's road plan from the ramparts of the Red Fort.

The Pradhan Mantri Gram Sadak Yojana, worth ₹60,000 crore, is meant to improve our rural connectivity.

However, irrigation has not been as lucky yet. My suggestion to the Central government is that it must set aside ₹50,000 crore for irrigation projects in various states. A mechanism must be formulated wherein the Central and state governments undertake irrigation projects on a 50:50 partnership, investing equal sums of money.

In Maharashtra, for example, if the state and Central governments put in ₹7,000 crore each, then in five years, most problems of the farmers will be taken care of. Of course, each penny disbursed thus will have to be accounted for, to prevent its misuse. This way, several irrigation projects in the state will soon become a reality. If the government undertakes this irrigation plan, then the drought-affected areas will bear a different look in five years' time.

Preventing the misuse of relief funds and addressing the issue of irrigation is the key to solving the problem of farmers' suicides. I will go to the extent of saying that the Central Bureau of Investigation (CBI) should hold an enquiry to unravel the cases of fraud that have taken place, especially in misusing the Prime Minister's and Chief Minister's packages for Vidarbha. Similarly, there are other frauds like well-off families getting duplicate Below the Poverty Line (BPL) certificates. This malpractice, again, has enjoyed the patronage of politicians. The result of all this has been that the condition of farmers, in Vidarbha and other drought-affected belts across the country, continues to worsen. The death toll keeps increasing, instead of decreasing.

Corruption is not an unusual phenomenon in our country but the level and extent of corruption in relief packages that are meant to save poor lives is bound to make any well-meaning Indian hang his head in shame.

The time has come to go all out and fix this menace.

A Futuristic Approach to Welfare

I had an opportunity to present a proposal on an issue that is equally crucial to the standard of living of our people, both in urban and rural areas. This vital issue can transform the life of the poor. At the same time, it can solve the problem of mushrooming slums in urban areas.

As I have mentioned, Vajpayeeji had formed a committee for making tarred roads in rural areas across the country. I was assigned the responsibility of heading this committee. While studying about all these regions, I observed that if we could plant trees on both sides of the tarred roads and float a plantation employment scheme alongside, this would generate employment for more than 5 million rural youth.

The adoption of biotechnology and organic farming is another aspect that presents a huge opportunity for us. We import chemical fertilisers from many countries. Many of our companies manufacture a variety of pesticides and fertilisers for which they need to import raw material from abroad. As a result, a huge amount of foreign currency flows out of the country. If the crops are produced using organic manure and biotechnology, the production of grains, vegetables and other varieties of crops will increase effectively, besides reducing the cost.

Hence, the use of organic manure, biofertilisers and bioinsecticides should be emphasised. If the same are to be produced by our farmers, then neem seeds will prove to be very useful. Many people have tried processing cow urine to produce manure. For instance, a scientist in Nagpur-based Go-Vigyan Anusandhan Kendra had prepared concentrates of cow urine. Processing it with *kaduneem* (commonly known in English as bead tree/Chinaberry), he sprinkled it on cotton pests to obtain successful results. Such unconventional experiments have been successful in our country. However, as they have been carried out individually or in small clusters, these experiments have not yielded optimum results.

If we just consider Maharashtra, the total geographical area of the state is approximately 307 lakh hectares, out of which only 80 lakh hectares of land is used for agriculture. A total of 225 lakh hectares of land is infertile, uneven and bumpy. Many NGOs have experimented successfully with plantation and related projects in Pune and Sangli districts. A report submitted by the renowned environmentalist, Mohan Dharia, for wasteland development was a particularly useful step in this direction. I have elaborated upon this report's key points in the chapter on wasteland management.

Any successful project requires three components: Awakening, training and inventing. I am happy that, in recent years, our farming sector has seen some positive changes. Our farmers are better informed and better travelled than farmers of the previous generation. Increased exposure has influenced their outlook positively.

Today, fruits and vegetables are exported on a very large scale. For instance, grapes worth about ₹278 crore are exported from Nasik annually. Similarly, pomegranates and berries are exported from Solapur. Farmers have directly benefitted from this change. We need to see how we can increase the fertility of the land, and also build confidence in the global market by using biotechnology and biofertilisers. There is no doubt that we have this capacity.

A few years ago, I had visited Israel. As I have always been keenly interested in rural agriculture, I was there for a few days to study some of their latest advancements in farming. Israel has dry, Mediterranean climate with scant rainfall. Yet, with all their limitations, they have created miracles on infertile land while we have not created anything similar despite having a regular, robust monsoon season. Israel's achievements, thus, are exemplary. Israel's agricultural produce are in good demand throughout the world.

SOCIAL FORESTRY

I would like to present a fresh thought here. The forest department in Maharashtra has 65 lakh hectares of land, out of which 28 lakh hectares is in Vidarbha. Approximately 40 lakh hectares of the forest department's land is barren. To plant fruit bearing trees, flowers or fruits in a hectare of land or even to make the land fertile, the minimum expenditure required is approximately ₹20,000. If 40 lakh hectares of land is being planted, the expense would bc ₹8,000 crorc. Taking into account the land of the forest department, Maharashtra has a total of 145 lakh hectares of infertile land. If this entire chunk of infertile land is to be made green, or if medicinal plants are to be planted or if the area is to be converted into a 'forest area', what will be the total investment required for the purpose? I have not calculated this, but possibly, the required funds would be around ₹29,000 crore. Is it feasible to go ahead with such a high investment? I am aware that if this huge task is to be undertaken under a government scheme, then the results are bound to be unsatisfactory. I know how a government scheme works. The officials show different expenditure figures in black and white, different from the actual ones. Owing to this scenario, often a mere 10 to 12 per cent of the actual work gets completed. The scheme does not reach the poor.

As far-fetched as it may seem, the challenge over here lies in trying to explore if we can involve the private sector in this initiative.

Whenever we prepare a scheme, we must estimate the amount of investment, its interest amount, the profits and the gestation period in order to arrive at the Internal Rate of Return (IRR). When I was a minister in Maharashtra for four and a half years, I had said on a number of occasions that the Mumbai-Pune Expressway will not require a rupee. People were not convinced, but my promise was backed by logic.

My logic is simple: If we involve the private sector, instead of using the government funds, it will have a big advantage—it will generate enhanced employment opportunities. My calculation says that, on an average, for an investment of ₹1,000 crore, 100,000 people should get employment. Coming back to the issue of infertile and sub-fertile land, I would like to reiterate that we have the required technology and we are in a position to carry out experiments to increase the fertility of our farming land. Tribal people ought to be employed in this task. Large sections of our tribal population do not have opportunities for work. They end up coming to Mumbai, Nagpur and Aurangabad and survive on trash, because they have no other option.

Let me give another example. The cultivation of *tendu* leaves (mainly used in manufacturing beedi), in the district of Gadchiroli, can generate an annual revenue of roughly ₹100 crore for the government. Considering that this area has witnessed huge disturbances in recent years due to the Naxal problem, the volume of production of *tendu* leaves has not been very impressive. We need to work out a plan to engage the tribals actively in the agricultural sector. Or else, they will continue to grope in despair and become prey to the Naxal menace.

Similarly, encouraging bamboo plantation can work wonders for us. We have huge stretches of infertile land which can be used for bamboo plantation, thereby employing many people. Bamboo is commonly found in our forests and it has many uses, especially in the construction industry. Bamboo is pressed to make laminating boards which are used worldwide.

In China, for instance, the government has invested heavily in developing bamboo products into an industry. In every bamboo manufacturing unit, on an average, eighty tribals can be employed. If we give more impetus to the bamboo industry, it will emerge as a big employment generator in tribal areas.

The rural areas have a lot of potential which needs to be tapped in every possible way. However, at times, it is irrational for the government to invest huge amounts in formal industry, especially when the estimated returns are not found to be commensurate with the proposed investment. In this situation, alternatives such as leveraging the bamboo industry need to be considered more seriously.

CLOSE TO MY HEART

Coming back to the plantation employment scheme, let me explain my proposal in detail. This scheme is the closest to my heart as even the educated unemployed will gain employment opportunities from this.

If, say, 50 km of land comes under plantation, then, after a few years, every ten people living in that stretch of land will get ₹2-3 lakh per year from it. On roads connecting two villages, trees should be planted on both the sides, stretching up to 4 km. The maintenance cost will occur in the first two to three years. But, after a few years, the produce can be shared by the youth employed in the programme and the Gram Panchayat. This money can be used for the development of the village. The national highways and district highways should also be planted with trees in the same way and in just eight to ten years, the value of these trees will grow many times over.

Let me specifically give you the example of the teak tree. If you plant a teak tree, then after ten to fifteen years, each tree will be worth ₹2-4 lakh. Teak wood has huge demand in the country. Teak tree plantation should also be considered from the viewpoint of employment generation, ecology and also from the commercial point of view. By commercial, I do not mean we must involve corporates in it. If the infertile land with a private individual has to be made ready for production, the investment required for this would be approximately ₹20,000 per hectare. The person must have funds to work on this. If we plant trees, employment will be created on a large scale and agricultural export will increase. Biofertilisers, bioinsecticides and biopesticides will be manufactured. The fertilisers from leaves and plant will be made to replace chemical fertilisers. This will also increase the production in the rural sector. Per capita income and GDP will increase. Youth will get employment at their native place instead of migrating to cities. This will increase their spending capacity, ultimately encouraging the industries. Besides, it will reduce the growing problem of slums in cities.

When I was the PWD minister in Maharashtra, I travelled extensively across the state to personally oversee the various construction projects. Whenever I travelled to the Konkan region, I found it fascinating to drive down roads that were adorned with Alphonso mango trees on both sides. I guess, being a foodie, seeing delicious fruit in close proximity had its charm for me. But more than that, I felt very happy to see the prosperity those trees brought to the people of the region.

An idea struck me thus: Why can't the government step into the picture and institutionalise mango plantation in the region? A step forward would be to plant these mango trees in government guest houses. Another way could be to invite farmers owning more than 10-12 acres of land to collaborate with the government. The government could provide financial support to these farmers to grow such plantations more professionally and in a more focussed manner. This would also provide employment to the youth of the region. If the government comes forward and pursues an organised plantation scheme, it would yield huge revenues for the state, which can be used for the overall development of the region.

I would like to point out here that independent organisations have attempted tree plantation schemes in isolation. For instance, in Sangli, 50,000 pomegranate trees were planted a few years ago. A similar experiment was conducted in Nagpur. An organisation named Vanrai had championed plantations and orchards in places like Pune, Mumbai and Nasik. These voluntary organisations have done a good job but they have their own limitations. If we want to make the infertile land fertile on a national scale, it will require a huge amount of sustained investment and perseverance, which is where a direct role of the government becomes important.

The only note of caution here is the need for transparency. There have been instances where a well-placed industrialist often applies for 1,000 hectares of land which is assigned to him instantly, without even carefully scrutinising the proposal. Such practices should be avoided. State governments need to be more responsible and discerning in denotifying land and selling it. If, after proper evaluation, the government is convinced about the feasibility of the proposal in respect of the unused land, it should go ahead. If the government does not want to give it to a particular corporate house, calling for tenders is always advisable. If someone comes up with an offer to invest, say, ₹500 crore in this way and says he will use the most modern techniques in agriculture, will set up a good laboratory for R&D purposes, etc., then this type of investment will create employment opportunities. Hence, my sincere request to all state governments is that they prepare a plantation employment scheme for all such infertile lands.

Similarly, a concrete plan needs to be drawn to earmark the green belts along the national and state highways as well as railway routes. It is important to meticulously decide the distribution of every hectare of land. A transparent process should be designed for the plantation employment scheme, as it has the potential to yield us crores of rupees without a significant investment. Unused, idle or infertile lands also need to be given due care, as these require lot of attention. We must prepare effective schemes that will provide a solution for ecological as well as employment issues, besides resulting in increase in state and national revenues.

Traditional Indian knowledge and systems are gaining worldwide acceptance today. For instance, Ayurveda is becoming increasingly popular, 'herbal' products are in demand everywhere. We can, thus, earmark huge chunks of land for Ayurveda plantations in various states, including those stretches that have so far been considered infertile. We will have to draw up a comprehensive plan for this, adopting the most competitive and professional approach. We need not take the shorter route of directing this scheme to any industrialist. We can issue bonds in this scheme if the need arises. Different categories of people can thus invest in this. Even the Central government can extend various concessions. However, the implementation of this scheme requires a high level of transparency. Otherwise, giant industrial houses may participate in this scheme just for their own advantage. The scheme should also be leak-proof. It should be planned considering the welfare of the poor.

GAON CHALO

In keeping with our focus on rural India, in my tenure as the party president, I made *Gaon Chalo* (Go to Villages) the slogan of the BJP, with its new vision of technology for *gramodaya* (village development).

Ending the systemic neglect of agriculture and rural development has to be the first requirement of an alternative economic model for India. The foremost requirement today is to redesign government policies to ensure a massive flow of public and private investments into agriculture and rural infrastructure.

Capital should be made available to farmers and rural entrepreneurs at low cost and on easy terms. This can help augment land and water resources, set up value-added agro-processing units and develop new high-yielding farm practices, including organic farming. A number of rural infrastructure development works can be taken out of inefficient government departments and entrusted to rural entrepreneurs and farmers' bodies with people's supervision.

Rural areas should have the same priority for power supply as urban areas.

Here, I would like to emphasise another important requirement of an alternative development and governance model. In spite of the Congress party's tall claims of the Seventy-third and Seventy-fourth Constitutional Amendments, there has been no effective financial and administrative empowerment of Panchayati Raj institutions and municipal bodies. I am, therefore, of the view that at least 10 per cent of the Central tax revenues should be transferred directly to Gram Panchayats and municipal bodies. Similarly, funds under the Special Component Plan for the Scheduled Castes and Tribal Sub-Plan for the Scheduled Tribes should be properly allocated for the welfare of these communities and utilised with their democratic participation.

In unleashing rural India's growth potential, we ought to shed the mechanical approach we have had so far and adopt an innovative approach. For example, encouragement to rural and wildlife tourism in certain tribal areas of the country has encouraged local entrepreneurs to build better infrastructure in the regions.

The vision of *Gaon Chalo* is to see rural India bloom,

with the provision of good roads and public transport, world-class telecom and IT facilities, 24×7 power supply, availability of pre-cooling plants and cold storages near markets, water and other basic needs, efficient financial services and market connectivity. This will attract new types of high-skilled and high-value enterprises to rural India. The new advances in IT, biotechnology, nanotechnology and energy-saving and material-saving sciences in the twenty-first century indeed hold the promise of decentralising and dispersing production and other economic activities. The compulsions of environment protection have made this a global imperative. Therefore, all our policies should be geared to hasten this transformation.

Not only should we stem distress migration of rural populations to urban areas, but also create conditions for urban people to go and live in India's modern hi-tech villages.

Similarly, we need to have effective steps in place to end the agony of unorganised labourers, which again is a burgeoning problem in the Indian context.

Rural India has suffered due to neglect in the last sixty-six years. The twenty-first century is the time to correct this imbalance and make our villages the leaders of new India.

Purti and Social Entrepreneurship

The essence of an agro-centric Indian spirit lies in her villages. More than eight lakh big or small villages contribute to make India the vibrant country that she is. These villages form the lifeline through which the great Indian cultural, spiritual, social and economic heritage flows. To understand the real spirit of India, one has to understand the spirit of these villages.

We are surging ahead in the twenty-first century. India is a torchbearer of the massive progress and change that the world is witnessing today. We are fast racing towards a situation that shall see India as a developed country. But the standards of success remain unbalanced or constrained in many spheres. This imbalance badly hampers the all-round development of the nation. Under-developed villages impose a burden on the development of cities and make them weak. Lack of proper industrial policies and long-lasting developmental plans grossly impede the overall development of the country. This gap has led to a steep rise in unemployment in villages as well as in cities—besides the unfortunate spate of suicides—resulting in an irrelevant education system, lack of basic infrastructure like power, roads, water and land for upcoming industries.

We need to turn to villages if we have to alleviate these problems and achieve sustainable, all-round development for the country. It is imperative that we direct the flow of development towards the villages in the country. If every village is equipped with agro-based and agro-produce industry, it will lead to a long and strong chain of employment generation. Infinite opportunities for self-employment can be created through small-scale and cottage-sector industries. This goal can be achieved by using advanced technology, imparting professional, vocational training to convert the abundantly available rural raw material and manpower into a successful economic business model.

FINDING A NEW MEANING IN LIFE

It was with this vision in mind that in the year 2000, I started the Purti Group of companies. The group is creating employment and development opportunities for lakhs of youth in Vidarbha through its active interests in sugar, energy, biodiesel, cottage industries, dairy and agro-processing industrial units.

A few months after I had started Purti, I met with a life-threatening accident when my car had a head-on collision with another vehicle. The accident was so devastating that I was bedridden for almost a year, barely able to move my limbs. In the early phase, even my chances of recovery had seemed bleak.

When you go through such a life-altering phase, you're bound to come out a changed person. At least, I experienced that in my life. Nitin Gadkari was a different person before and after the accident. I learnt to appreciate the simple joys of living even more. My political ambitions almost died with the accident. Instead, what emerged was a greater desire to utilise my remaining life to work for the betterment of the downtrodden. An inner voice told me that there was a larger purpose attached to me getting a lifeline. It was a calling that I had to answer.

From that point onwards, the driving force behind all my entrepreneurship objectives has been to improve the living conditions of the poor. I am, thus, a politician who became an entrepreneur rather than an entrepreneur who used his clout to enter politics. And there was a clear thought process that guided my decision.

I have always believed that it is important for a politician to realise his social responsibilities. I belong to the Vidarbha region where poverty, along with governmental apathy, has led to a very pitiable situation for farmers. Year after year, instead of improving, the scenario has gone from bad to worse. In such circumstances, one cannot depend on the government alone.

I believe that after God and government, there is you.

When the government is found wanting, it is time for capable and well-meaning individuals to take extra initiative and compensate for the government's deficiencies. In other words, as Gandhiji had put it, 'Be the change that you wish to see in the world.' That is precisely what I did by taking the lead in setting up this organisation. The sole purpose was to generate employment in the region and to try and bring an industrious work culture to rural areas.

In Vidarbha, even though the climate is not conducive for

sugarcane production, there is a small stretch where sugarcane is grown. In 2000, I set up a sugar mill, disregarding the advice of many friends who cautioned me about the difficulties. With experience, I was to realise that making a sugar industry work in the region was indeed akin to walking on fire.

But I was not one to lose heart. Instead, I decided to diversify the business into a co-generation plant where the by-products of one unit would be used for the production of another product. Once again, people scoffed at my idea. But I was determined.

The massive electricity deficit in the region provided us an opportunity. I decided to produce electricity by using bagasse, which is the fibrous matter that remains after sugarcane stalks are crushed to extract their juice. We produced electricity alternately from coal and bagasse for captive use. This reduced our dependence on coal. At the same time, another by-product of sugar, molasses, was used to produce ethanol and alcohol. Ethanol was then used to produce biodiesel.

The Purti Group has been the first to employ the co-generation technique in Vidarbha. What is most satisfying for me is that these initiatives have addressed two of my greatest social concerns: Today, the Purti Group produces 33 MW of electricity, which is a big boon for the region. Secondly, it has taken the lead in biofuel and shown that the resources of the farm sector can be gainfully employed in the power and energy sector.

Honesty is the biggest capital of the twenty-first century. With sincere efforts and integrity, anything is possible. That is what the success of the Purti Group in the last ten years has proved. Rural development has always been at the centre of my industrial programmes. I firmly believe that rural progress through rural development will lead to our nation's growth. I have always asked the people to bring about their own and their neighbours' progress through self-help and not depend on the government for each and every thing. Everybody knows the importance of self-help, but few act upon it.

The doors of progress can be opened by a simple formula: Use of urban wealth and infrastructure by expert business professionals to bring about tenable progress in rural areas. We have proved this through successful management of the Purti Group. Our various businesses have brought a sea change in the lives of nearly 250,000 people in Nagpur, Bhandara and Wardha districts. The Purti Group not only provides inspiration but also provides assistance to people of other districts of Vidarbha to establish financially competent and socially inspired industries.

Knowledge is of no use if it is not transmitted or shared. Moreover, our society needs right role models and sources of inspiration. I have always believed and tried to give something back to the society that I grew up in. I would ideally wish that educated and professionally qualified youth from backward regions sacrifice the comfort of cities and come back to the smaller towns and villages where they grew up. These individuals can set up agriculture-based industries and help instill a sense of enterprise in fellow villagers who, for various reasons, have been left behind. This will lead to the development of the community as a whole.

INNOVATIONS

The Purti Group has launched some very innovative social initiatives, the most notable among which is solar fencing.

Solar fencing is an ambitious project initiated by us to protect crops from wild animals and thieves. As the name suggests, this fencing involves wiring that operates on solar energy. Besides, the low voltage it produces is also not strong enough to seriously injure anyone. The expenditure incurred in installing the solar fence is 50 per cent less than the conventional fence.

At first, the cost of fencing one acre of land by this technique came to ₹1 lakh but as we managed to convince more and more farmers to adopt it, the cost came down drastically. For instance, the cost of fencing five acres of land comes to only ₹2 lakh. Moreover, it is now acknowledged that solar fencing can go a long way in assisting farmers in the most backward belt of Vidarbha.

Apart from this, the group has undertaken manufacturing of solar cells for generating solar energy. They are being sold at the cost of ₹7,200 and the group has already obtained orders worth over ₹1 crore. These cells can run without any problem for a minimum of five years and can revolutionise life in the most backward areas of the country, where electricity is still not available.

The group has also been a pioneer in promoting biodiesel in Maharashtra. It has undertaken the commendable step towards producing electricity from forest produce. The adivasis (tribal people) of Gondia, Chandrapur, Gadchiroli and Bhandara benefit from this. The seeds of *erandi*, *karanji*, *moha*, *saal* and *ratnajyoti*, collected by them, are bought by the Purti Group for making biodiesel. Apart from this, biodiesel can also be made by processing palm oil and soya bean oil. Our biodiesel production machinery, with a capacity of producing 3000 LPD, is an important step in the direction of saving foreign exchange. Most of the produced biodiesel is used in our own manufacturing processes. The remaining fuel is sold to the public at a reduced rate.

Scientists in India are working on the advanced technology of running engines on ethanol. This may soon be the fuel of choice for all vehicles. With this aim, we have produced Ener-diesel, a product developed by mixing ethanol and diesel. All the vehicles of the Purti Group run successfully on this fuel, which saves both the environment as well as foreign exchange, thus doing a great service to the country.

When one grows up negotiating shortages and limitations of multiple kinds, the best thing it does is that it teaches one to make optimal use of scarce resources available. I guess this must have been the psychology that continuously drove me to explore multiple and simultaneous use of the various resources available to me. I would like to talk about an innovation we carried out recently.

As part of the manufacturing process in our distilleries, 33,000 cubic metres of methane used to be heated in boilers. Instead of heating the methane, we decided to experiment, compress and clean up the large quantity of methane. The results were outstanding. The process led to the production of 18,000 kg of Compressed Natural Gas (CNG). The other by-products obtained in the process were 13,000 cubic metres of carbon dioxide (CO_2) and hydrogen sulphide (H_2S).

We then collaborated with the National Environmental Engineering Research Institute (NEERI), Nagpur, to further process and utilise this CO_2 to help in algae farming (plants breathe in the carbon dioxide and release oxygen during their growth). This algae was then used to make biodiesel. Similarly, H_2S can be utilised to produce enough sulphur that would make 150 kg of pesticides.

At the Purti Group, we have installed two rice husk process units, each having a 12 MW electricity generation capacity. Rice hull (husk) contains 20 per cent silica. So the ash obtained from burnt rice husk is a good source of silica. If 350 tonnes of rice husk goes through the flash combustion process in a temperature and pressure controlled gasifier, it will yield roughly 140 tonnes of ash. This ash can be processed in the separator to produce 18 tonnes of silica. The silicon thus produced, is used in solar cells.

Increased availability of affordable solar cells is the most effective way to promote solar energy usage.

I am happy to inform you that a group of twenty journalists from the North Eastern states of Arunachal Pradesh and Manipur visited the Vidarbha region in April 2012 to study some of the rural development initiatives that the Purti Group has undertaken. This team was particularly impressed with the use of bio-waste for power generation and innovative reusage of water and has urged their respective state governments to emulate the Purti model of rural development and human empowerment.

Given our social commitment, to the extent possible, the Purti Group likes to spend on charity. Our special concern is for the poor heart and cataract patients. Whenever we come across cases where people require financial assistance, we try to extend assistance to them. I wish to reiterate that every responsible citizen of this country must realise his social responsibility. In whatever capacity possible, one must try to make at least a part of the benefits enjoyed by him, available to people lower down the social order.

Rome was not built in a day. Similarly, none of the initiatives undertaken by me were accomplished in a day. I have gone through multiple failures. But those setbacks could not weaken my determination. When I started the sugar factory near Nagpur, everybody was cynical. They had a point. All sugar factories had shut down in the area. But, through sheer hard work and determination, I was able to prove the cynics wrong. The Purti Group now owns another sugar mill, the Mahatma Sugar and Power Ltd, which had closed down.

With the work that the group has done in improving the lives of rural people in the Vidarbha region, I can say this with happiness and satisfaction that we have lived up to the ideals of

Pandit Deendayal Upadhyaya. His thoughts and philosophy are the guiding force for me and my workers.

While I have done a few things, a lot still needs to be done. I have been repeatedly pressing the government to encourage the use of biofuel in our country. I can see a future when a significant fraction of our agricultural workforce will be doing their bit in making a biotechnology revolution in our country a reality. Biotechnology has opened up a whole new avenue for our farming community and I can assure you that the Purti Group will only increase its efforts in the coming years to provide employment to more and more farmers.

Men are mortal. So are ideas. An idea needs propagation as much as a plant needs watering. Otherwise both will wither and die.

— Babasaheb Ambedkar

FIVE

Urban Infrastructure

American roads are good not because America is rich; America is rich because American roads are good.

—John F Kennedy

The Mumbai-Pune Expressway: A Case Study

Certain achievements become a benchmark in your life, so much so that even years or decades later, you are known for that particular achievement. The Mumbai-Pune Expressway is one such achievement that always precedes my introduction.

The Expressway continues to be among the most significant infrastructural advancements made in post-Independence India. What people cherish most is the fact that it has reduced travel time between Mumbai and Pune from 4-5 hours to 2 hours—the most tangible benefit experienced by anyone who has travelled on the Expressway. However, the real benefits are so vast that they can perhaps never be estimated in actual terms.

The Expressway has led to the expansion of both Mumbai and Pune. So, today, while Panvel on the Mumbai side is a mini-city of its own, Wakad and Hinjewadi on the Pune side have also seen huge industrial expansion. Trade between the two cities has grown. People who are connected to both cities prefer to live on the outer suburbs of either city. All this has led to newer employment opportunities. At the same time, it provides the city of Mumbai, which is surrounded by water on three sides, a scope for de-congestion.

For me personally, the Mumbai-Pune Expressway is history. Though I am happy I could give the people of Mumbai and Pune this prized gift, I prefer to live in the present and talk about the future. But, for the sake of my newer friends, I shall do a quick recap of how we made that dream project a reality. The reason I dwell on it here is to let the younger generation know that despite all limitations imposed by the system, political will has the power to overcome odds.

When I became the PWD minister in Maharashtra in 1995, I realised that it was a godsend to reverse many of the failings relating to our ill-equipped road infrastructure.

But I was faced with a major handicap: The total annual budget of the PWD ministry for its various construction projects was just ₹750 crore. Besides, there was a huge backlog of incomplete projects, whose costs had escalated manifold. I, thus, had two options before me: One was to spend my five-year tenure merely cooling my heels and trying to complete the previous projects. The other was to explore unconventional means and set an example for the future. I knew the task would not be completed even in 350 years if I only depended upon the allotted amount of money. Unconventional, out-of-the-box thinking was needed to generate the funds necessary for the purpose.

My quest for solutions had me accompanying the then Chief Minister of Maharashtra, Manohar Joshi, on a tour of Southeast Asia. We visited Malaysia during the tour. We were scheduled to meet the then Prime Minister of Malaysia, Mahathir Mohammad. Prior to the meeting, we assembled in a hall where some of the officials of the Malaysian government were also present. On their request, we saw a twenty-minute film on the development schemes of their country before we met their Prime Minister. While we watched the film titled *Malaysia Economic Planning 2012*, we were also given a book to read. The film and the book revealed how perfectly the government had planned the development of the country, encapsulating various areas such as sports, economy, transport, farm, industry and business sectors, right till 2012. Indeed, the planning was quite impressive. Later, during the meeting with the Prime Minister, I was particularly impressed with his vision of development and strategies to overcome the problems and difficulties. I felt that this vision to translate these plans into reality with firm political willpower, had secured a bright future for Malaysia.

I could feel the confidence accompanying every thought of theirs and I felt that this was their biggest capital. Political will is indeed the greatest capital behind the progress of any state or nation. It is more important than funds, technology and human resources. The Malaysia visit was, thus, a huge learning experience for me, which gave me a new direction to think.

It was from the Malaysians that I learnt of the PPP model, known as BOT, for executing development projects. This concept, popular in Western countries, was frowned upon by Indian politicians until then. When we finally adopted it, this not only made the major arterial roads connecting Maharashtra better and well-maintained, but also helped release huge amounts of budget funds earmarked for such roads, to be utilised for rural road development. The concept was instrumental in making the Mumbai-Pune Expressway and fifty-five flyovers in Mumbai a reality, in record time. The Bandra-Worli Sea Link was also conceived during my tenure.

When I returned to Mumbai, I started working specifically on the Mumbai-Pune Expressway and the various schemes related to the building of flyovers in the city. The investment for flyovers required nearly ₹1,800 crore and the Express Highway would have cost ₹2,000 crore. It was next to impossible to execute this within the ambit of existing budgets. After examining various options, I set up the Maharashtra State Road Development Corporation (MSRDC) to expedite these projects. I was the chairman of this organisation.

Considering the magnitude of the projects, the initial going remained tough. We had two divergent viewpoints on whether the Expressway project should have been handed to the MSRDC. As a first step, we had followed the conventional way of inviting tenders for the project. Reliance Industries submitted to us a much-inflated tender worth ₹3,200 crore. We submitted the tender to ICICI Bank for examination. They too noted their reservations about the quoted figure and some other clauses.

Finally, in a cabinet meeting where we discussed the Reliance proposal, I stuck my neck out and refused to accept it. Accepting such an inflated tender would have implied giving in to exploitation of both the government and the shareholders.

Subsequently, I decided to hand over the project to MSRDC—being a new entity it did not have a balance sheet to vouch for its credibility. But, then, I was willing to support the new entity rather than be stuck in the conventional rigmarole. MSRDC's CEO, Ramesh Chandra Sinha, sought government guarantee against the loan that he would raise from the market, which I happily facilitated. And, thus, began our tryst with history.

I find it fascinating that some of the best ideas occur to you serendipitously. I remember that in those days, when we were wracking our brains trying to fix the right funding options, I had gone to a shop on Napean Sea Road in Mumbai to buy a TV set. I liked a particular TV set and was happy to know that it could be purchased in Equated Monthly Installments (EMIs) as well. Today, of course, every electronic gadget is available on easy EMIs but in those days such a thing was rare. After my interaction with the TV dealer, I ended up asking myself: If a TV can be purchased in EMIs, why can't roads be constructed with a similar investment-recovery pattern? The idea kept growing in my mind and eventually we did adopt the BOT model for the project.

I remember that I was invited by journalists in Pune for an interaction, just after the work on the Mumbai-Pune Expressway had begun. The Pune scribes started firing questions at me one after another. My condition was akin to a debutant Indian batsman facing the wrath of Aussie pacers on the bouncy tracks of Australia. Here's a sample of what the interaction was like:

> Question: What is the estimated value of funds that are required for constructing the Express Highway?
> Answer: ₹2,000 crore.
> Question: How about land acquisition?
> Answer: It has started and is moving with great speed. It will be completed in a couple of months.
> Question: What about environment clearance?
> Answer: We have received it.
> Question: How many tenders have been received?
> Answer: We are getting the tenders.

Question: You said that this work would require ₹2,000 crore, but Ambani's Reliance company had submitted a tender of ₹3,200 crore. What happened to that?

Answer: We have scrapped Reliance's tender because it was higher than what was actually required for this project. I am confident that we will be able to complete this project within ₹2,000 crore.

Question: How much funds do you already have?

I was at a loss for a reply to this question. If I told them the truth, I would have been caught on the wrong foot. But I have never lied to anybody in my life. So I told them point blank:

Answer: We have only ₹5 crore.

They all laughed when they heard my answer. One of them was sarcastic.

Question: Do you think that we journalists are here to listen to your wild imagination and write about it too?

Answer: No.

Question: Then how come you reject a tender of ₹3,200 crore, say that the work will be completed in ₹2,000 crore or even in ₹1,800 crore, and also claim that the work will be over within two years? Is there any basis for what you say? How are you going to complete this job in two years?

I was at the receiving end. I told them that while I agreed that I had only ₹5 crore with me, I would still assure them that the highway would be completed in two years' time. But my reply did not satisfy them.

Question: How will it be completed? From where will you get the money required to complete it?

Answer: If there is a will there is a way, if there is no will there are only surveys, discussions, seminars, committees, sub-committees and study groups. Because I have a strong willpower, I will complete this job within the stipulated time.

They left the venue, apparently not satisfied with my responses. The frown on their faces clearly indicated that they did not believe in what I said. Rather, they seemed confident that I would fail.

When I look back, the Mumbai-Pune Expressway and fifty-five flyovers of Mumbai, apart from being my most cherished accomplishments, hold tremendous significance in the history of India's infrastructural growth. These projects set a precedent not only for Maharashtra but for the entire country. It had a clear message for every leader and every bureaucrat in the country—integrity and willpower can defeat endless hurdles that come your way.

Fifteen years have gone by since. There has been a significant generational change—some of the key politicians, bureaucrats and journalists of those years are no longer that active; a younger generation has taken charge of governance and bureaucracy. For the benefit of those who may be interested in the execution of the Mumbai-Pune Expressway and the flyovers, I wish to recapitulate the key steps involved in the process as a case study.

BATTLING SCEPTICISM AND INFLATED BIDDING

Inspired by my Malaysia visit, I became obsessed with the Expressway project. I was determined to show the world that we can indeed build a world-class highway and in record time. I advocated the adoption of the BOT concept for this. However, despite all my attempts to reach out to the construction industry, both the industry and my own government seemed sceptical.

It is strange, but those who are low on determination and passion invariably tend to under-estimate those who possess these qualities. Many people have this tendency to shy away from path-breaking decisions and lead life the easy way. Such people demoralise others. Hence, my first battle was to fight the pessimism, scepticism and dismissive attitude of the people involved.

Undeterred, I went ahead with my plans. The PWD called for tenders for giving the Expressway on a BOT basis. Initially, there were five or six firms that had bought the tender documents. Eventually, however, all of them, including Reliance Industries and Hindustan Construction Company Ltd, formed a consortium and tendered a single bid. The bid was for ₹3,200 crore, almost two and a half times of what the Rail India Technical and Economic Services' estimate had been then. The bid also asked the government to agree to a whole host of conditions.

As someone who was increasingly fighting a lonely battle, I might as well have succumbed to the offer. However, allowing the cost to be inflated thus would have been unethical. We chose the harder way.

An individual's conviction needs to be stronger than the scepticism around him.

BIRTH OF MSRDC

Even as we grappled with different funding options without much breakthrough, in mid-1996, we toyed with the idea of creating an institution that would execute the project within the ambit of the state government, yet remain insulated from it. The idea was to execute the project through a wholly-owned corporation of the government, with no interference from the government.

After several rounds of discussion, we decided that this entity would be 100 per cent owned by the PWD, yet insulated from it in its functioning. It was also decided that unlike other government-owned corporations, the company would not have politicians or MLAs as directors. Instead, the board of directors would comprise professionals with reputation and credibility. Since fund raising was a critical aspect, it was also decided that at least a few of these directors would be people associated with large financial institutions.

As a first step, a government resolution was passed on 9 July 1996 and a new entity, MSRDC, was formed as a 100 per cent Government of Maharashtra undertaking under the PWD. It was incorporated as a limited company under the Companies Act 1956 on 2 August 1996, with an authorised capital of ₹5 crore.

On a broader note, I wish to question the appointment of politicians in most corporations that are set up by the Central and state governments in our country. Instead of politicians, we must have competent professionals, academicians, scientists and financial experts on these panels. This step will surely increase the efficiency and accountability of these corporations.

FINDING THE RIGHT MAN

The setting up of an entity like MSRDC was a historical step in India. However, it was just as critical for the organisation to have a CEO who was capable of leading it in the right direction.

We needed someone who was well versed in the working of the financial markets, had a previous record of meeting stiff challenges and had an unblemished record of personal integrity. After considering several names, we zeroed in on Ramesh Chandra Sinha, an IAS officer of the 1962 batch. What clinched the position for him was his performance as vice-chairman and managing director of the City and Industrial Development Corporation of Maharashtra Ltd (CIDCO) during 1990-94. Within one month of joining CIDCO, Sinha was told by the finance department that the corporation did not even have the money to pay salaries and that all available overdraft facilities had been exhausted.

Instead of using the easier route of approaching the government for funds, Sinha worked on his contacts with financial institutions to raise the funds. Among his major achievements were getting the Central Railway to extend the suburban harbour line train service to Navi Mumbai. This was the kind of dynamism that the CEO of MSRDC had to have.

I am not very famous as an orator, rather, I am infamous for my language. I recall an interaction with Sinha from those days. He explained the entire project to me and said that at least a five-year time frame would be required to complete this job. I knew his style of working. A very selfish thought crept into my mind, quite natural for a politician. I thought, if this Express Highway could be completed before the assembly elections of 1999, we would get some political benefit out of it. This thought grabbed my attention immediately and I told Sinha that we would have to complete this work within two years.

He reacted immediately, 'Sir, it is impossible.'

I asked him, who the minister was.

He said, 'You, sir.'

'Then who will take the decision?'

He replied with all humility, 'It is your authority to take the decision, sir.'

Then I issued an order to him, saying, 'Mr Sinha, I don't know anything except that this is the date of inauguration, two years hence. Do not give me any excuses, just do it.'

A visibly shaken Sinha responded, 'I will try my best, sir, I will try to do it, sir.'

In hindsight, I feel that getting the right CEO in place was the most critical decision. Had it been someone who was used to faltering on deadlines or someone who thought mechanically, I doubt whether we would have achieved our target in the stipulated time.

Identifying the right captain is half the game won. This identification process itself requires a lot of skill and diligence.

CONNECTIVITY WITHIN THE CITY

The Expressway between Panvel and Pune would have served little purpose if it was going to take two hours to reach Panvel from Mumbai. The most outspoken person on this issue was Madhav Jog, who ran one of the country's most reputed engineering firms, Jog Engineering. In January 1997, the Chief Minister appointed an expert committee headed by Jog to look into Mumbai's traffic problems. On 15 March 1997, the committee submitted a report recommending the construction of fifty-five flyovers to ease Mumbai's traffic woes. The report was accepted in totality.

Thus, these flyovers were to complement the Mumbai-Pune Expressway.

Today, a similar situation presents itself when we talk of the proposed new airport at Navi Mumbai. While the airport has been approved, we are way behind on the construction of the sea link between South Mumbai and Uran in Navi Mumbai.

When planning for giant projects like the Mumbai-Pune Expressway or the new airport in the present-day context, equal impetus has to be given to improving the connectivity to these points to derive optimal advantage of the new constructions.

AUTONOMY AND DELEGATION OF AUTHORITY

I was a student of economics. One of the examples I always give is the equation: $(A+B)^2= A^2 + B^2 + 2(AB)$. I often tell my colleagues, co-workers and friends to think positively. Together we can work in a better way. This positive thought and political will can jointly do wonders.

The pace at which the Mumbai-Pune Expressway and the

flyover projects were executed is a benchmark in India. Here are just a few indicators of how this pace was achieved:

- PWD consultants had started work on the Expressway alignment even before MSRDC was formed.
- As the MSRDC team was taking shape, the land acquisition process had already started.
- In order to make it more manageable, the Expressway project was divided into four sections and each of these was treated separately.
- Another innovative concept was the appointment of project management consultants to monitor the work.
- If MSRDC had not dealt with bureaucratic hurdles, even permission for storing explosives could have taken six months.
- Total scrutiny, including deciding the eligibility, marking on technical capability and verifying documents of fifty-five tenders was done in thirteen days and the work order issued.
- The decision to appoint project management consultants even before getting environmental clearance from the Union Ministry saved huge amount of time.
- Work orders were handed out at 10:30 a.m. on 1 January 1998, just hours before Parliament was dissolved and the model code of conduct came into place.
- Most significantly, individual contractors were given the freedom to take a call on all important matters, including minor changes in design, on the spot. The only things that needed approval from the MSRDC's CEO or chairman were the changes in cost and deadline.

An exhaustive mechanism needs to be in place to remove bottlenecks and obstacles, so that the actual construction work is carried out unhindered.

I can go on and on about the path-breaking initiatives that we had pursued for land acquisition, raising finances, importing world-class equipment, etc., but the thrust over here is merely to reiterate the enormous power of political will.

When the project was nearing completion, I was, once again, invited to a press conference in Pune. Before the interaction, the media was taken on a tour of the tunnels, roads, etc. which were under construction near Pune. When the press conference began, they were all surprised by the pace of completion of the project. They admitted they had not believed what I had said the last time. I then dwelt upon the making of the Mumbai-Pune Expressway in detail, emphasising that if we want to change the face of a town, district, state or even the country, a strong willpower is more important than all other resources.

You will be surprised but it is a fact that there were 22,000 people working in the PWD in the state and they could complete work worth ₹1,400 crore. As against that, the MSRDC completed the work worth ₹4,000 crore with just 48 employees in the same time period!

I wish to add here that I had sanctioned the Bandra-Worli Sea Link way back in 1997 when I was the PWD minister. At that time, the estimated cost of the project was ₹420 crore. As a result of the lethargy and mismanagement of the successive governments in Maharashtra, it was completed way behind schedule in 2009, by which time the project cost had gone up to a staggering ₹1,680 crore.

In hindsight, I feel our decision to adopt the BOT-PPP model was a giant leap forward for the entire country. In subsequent years it paved the way for several Central and state projects that had lain dormant for paucity of funds. This only reiterated my belief that India would have been a far more progressive model of growth, had we discarded our flawed model of Socialism some decades earlier.

New Challenges in Town Planning

Yeh hai Mumbai...

In a world that is shrinking by the day, top Indian cities are now global cities that showcase the health of the country's economy, even as they provide employment to millions of Indians who come from different parts of the country in search of a livelihood. The story is much the same with most large cities; so are the problems. However, let me once again base my thoughts on this subject with specific reference to India's financial capital, Mumbai.

There are several reasons why I choose Mumbai. One, Mumbai's challenges are the stiffest, considering it is surrounded by water on three sides. Therefore, limited area of expansion imposes even tougher demands on infrastructure as the population grows. Two, Mumbai is now a prized destination of world leaders who visit India to seek investments. That the Indian economy today is looked up to by many of our counterparts, makes it even more important that the city keeps pace with our growing clout as an economic powerhouse. Three, Mumbai is truly cosmopolitan in character as people from every part of the country come here in search of a livelihood. Moreover, despite its constraints, the city is extremely accommodating towards anybody who can match its energy and spirit. Therefore, Mumbai, in many ways, symbolises a mini-India. Finally, Mumbai holds a special place in my heart as, after Nagpur, this is the city where I have spent the maximum time.

Mumbai has much to offer, both to its own people and to the world. The opportunities and potential are enormous; it is a dynamic and vibrant metropolis, a busy international port, a natural hub with sea, air, road and rail links and a major centre of specialised educational, medical and cultural facilities. People from across the globe come here, making Mumbai their first stop, to meet corporate leaders and decision-makers before fanning out to other parts of the country.

The city plays a crucial role, with 70 per cent of all stock market transactions in the country taking place here. Mumbai's influence is huge; Pune, for instance, benefits immensely from its proximity to this city. In the last few years, Pune has been rapidly expanding, and much of its growth stems from the fact that it is often perceived as an extended suburb of Mumbai.

A CITY ON THE BRINK

Yet, there is the flip side. Rapid growth means a higher population density, and more people mean a greater burden on the city's infrastructure. Mumbai is restricted geographically; its area is only 4355 sq km, whereas according to the 2011 Census, the city has a density of over 20,000 people per sq km. This density also leads to a decaying social structure, with poverty levels rising, crime going up and anti-social elements bending the limits of the law. What makes it more difficult in the crush and thrust of the linear city is the fact that its central business district is at one end, with 70 per cent of jobs on the island, while most residents live in the suburbs—commuting for two to four hours daily in packed buses and local trains, just to get to their places of work.

The severe pressure on local trains has led many people to choose to travel in their own vehicles; on an average, the Eastern and Western Express Highways are used by more than 50,000 vehicles every day and over 70,000 vehicles cross the Sion-Panvel Highway daily. Every year, there is a 5 to 7 per cent rise in traffic, and with the load on public transportation, with aspiration levels going up and loans more easily available, owning a car today is no longer considered a luxury. In 1980, there were 286,132 vehicles in Mumbai, but by 2000, this figure had shot up to 910,728. In the years since, this figure has only gone up several notches. I am told that more than 350 new vehicles are registered in the Regional Transport Office (RTO) every day in Mumbai.

While these new vehicles have offered increased comfort to those unwilling to suffer unending traffic jams, they have also led to an alarming rise in pollution levels. An average of 620,000 people are affected every year due to air pollution in India and ₹4,500 crore are spent to treat the affected people. In Mumbai, 2.10 crore work days are lost due to pollution-related illnesses, 10 lakh people suffer from pollution related asthma, 7,000 people are admitted to hospital for pollution-related respiratory symptoms, while 28,000 adults and 250,000 children are affected by chronic bronchitis caused by pollution. More than ₹5,000 crore is spent on health damage costs in the city and every second child below three years is affected by lead pollution. Almost 86 per cent of this air pollution is due to vehicular exhaust.

THE TRANSPORT IMPERATIVE

There is much that needs to be done in Mumbai. There are many problems that need to be solved; the present infrastructure is simply insufficient to cater to the needs of this city's growing population.

The Mumbai Monorail project, for which work is underway as this book goes into print, should have been started many years ago. It needs to speed up in order to meet the deadline of the first service, which was supposed to start in 2011. The Mumbai Trans-Harbour Link (MTHL) and the JRD Tata Bridge to connect Nhava in Navi Mumbai and Sewri in Mumbai also need to be expedited. This will open new vistas for development on the mainland across the harbour, and promote future development in the east-west direction, thereby considerably reducing pressure on the city's road and rail network. The project, which will provide a road and rail link from Sewri to Nhava, involves construction of the 25 km long main bridge across the harbour and a traffic dispersal system at both the ends in the form of interchanges and elevated roads connecting the major arteries, both at the Mumbai city end and to the highways and the Mumbai-Pune Expressway.

Now that the Environment Ministry has cleared the international airport in Navi Mumbai, it becomes all the more important to improve the connectivity to Navi Mumbai. For this, the MTHL is a necessity which cannot be delayed any further.

In most of suburban Mumbai, travelling from the west to east or vice versa at any given time is an extremely painstaking process due to overcrowded flyovers and narrow subways. These should be supplemented by the construction of flyovers, Road Over Bridges (ROBs) and two-tier elevated roads on all heavily-crowded existing roads, subways and underpasses for light vehicles and pedestrians.

The public transport system must be strengthened at all levels. Over the years, various options were studied: The Light Rail Transit System (LRTS), the Mass Rapid Transport System (MRTS), the sky bus system, the aero bus, a metro rail, electric vans and buses. Now that the construction of the monorail and sky bus project is underway in full swing, they need to be expedited so that Mumbaikars get a reprieve from their traffic woes.

Mumbaikars often spend just as long commuting to their places of work from the stations as they do in the trains themselves, thus adding to the pressure on the city's road network. Railway stations must be modernised and reconstructed on a BOT basis and the constructed space should be fully exploited commercially.

I am disappointed to note that even after the 2006 serial blasts, the 26/11 terrorist shootout at the Chhatrapati Shivaji Terminus and then the 13/7 multiple explosions, absolutely nothing has been done to improve security at local train stations. The modernised and reconstructed railway stations need to give due importance to security. If we need to hike the train fares by ₹1 for this, so be it.

Travelling in local trains during peak hours is a nightmare due to the overcrowding; travelling in buses is a pain during rush hours, the journey could well take three hours, by which time you can reach Pune instead. Is there a third option?

While the existing road and rail network is being augmented, one area of transport has strangely been neglected, in a city that is one of India's largest ports. While places like Hong Kong have used waterways to their advantage, Mumbai has given little thought to this area, apart from making a few sporadic attempts to introduce it. Special emphasis must be placed on waterways; a special purpose vehicle with private participation for water transport projects is long overdue. Indigenous barges, hovercraft and boats must be built for both public and goods transport, particularly with imported technical backup. Jetties and parking lots must be constructed to facilitate water transport. The whole effort should be to make this mode of transport efficient, economical and compatible with suburban trains.

TACKLING POLLUTION

Pollution takes many forms in this city, with both air and noise pollution coming together to make life unbearable for the average Mumbaikar. All industries contributing to air pollution must be relocated; this will cause some heartburn and lead to protests, but the same can be avoided if special concessions are given to entrepreneurs. The three largest cities in India, Mumbai, Delhi and Chennai, are among the world's most polluted cities.

More than 40,000 people in these cities die annually because of polluted air, according to a World Bank 1995 study.

The air in Indian cities is so harmful that it is equivalent to smoking twenty cigarettes a day. Likewise, Indian rivers are highly polluted from discharges of industrial and municipal waste. This indiscriminate disposal of urban refuse has resulted in land pollution as well.

It is not just the large industries that contribute to this state of affairs. Every vehicle on the road makes the situation worse. Stringent norms are required and must be implemented and eco-friendly fuels should be increasingly used in the cities. In Mumbai, all existing buses and trucks must be converted to CNG/LPG by providing sufficient filling facilities and new buses should run on environment-friendly fuels. Light vehicles and two and three-wheelers should be encouraged to run on CNG/LPG, and vehicles older than fifteen years should not be allowed to ply unless they are converted into CNG/LPG vehicles. The use of public transport facilities and sharing of vehicles should be encouraged.

Noise pollution can be just as dangerous as air pollution. It is vital to create sound control barriers at heavy traffic points and ensure that no-noise zones are created around hospitals, schools and residential areas. Power horns and sirens must be banned and Public Announcement (PA) systems upgraded. National and international norms on sound and air pollution should be strictly enforced in Mumbai. All this can only be done if public awareness is created and if each one of us resolves to make a difference.

The trucks plying on the city roads are another major cause of traffic jams in Mumbai. Their movement is essential for the city to survive, but alongside, it is imperative to construct new terminals for these heavy vehicles on the outskirts of the city.

These terminals can come up on Mumbai-Ahmedabad, Mumbai-Nasik, Mumbai-Goa and Mumbai-Pune highways and facilities at the Wadala Truck Terminal should be upgraded, including multiple-axle vehicle parking, repair facilities and CNG fuel stations.

While many of these initiatives have been implemented in Delhi and some other cities, several other cities which are far more polluted and choked have lagged behind enormously, exposing a vast chunk of our population to major health hazards. There is, therefore, an urgent need to adopt a uniform approach across the country to combat pollution and traffic woes.

A Third Mumbai!

My vision for the flyovers and Expressway, however, goes far beyond the immediate transport needs of a burgeoning city. I believe that, with Mumbai having reached choking point, and its counter magnet Navi Mumbai growing rapidly, it is time to think of a Third Mumbai—a green and corporate city to be planned and developed in consultation with internationally reputed planners and architects to cater to the future needs of Mumbai.

This Third Mumbai, linked to South Mumbai through the new flyovers, would be spread across a 360 sq km area between Uran and Panvel, providing fast track connectivity with all the airports and ports. It will also be connected with Mumbai through the Nhava-Sewri MTHL and with Navi Mumbai.

I believe that it should house the Central and state government offices, including Vidhan Bhavan, Mantralaya and the courts; the stock exchange, corporate houses, multinational corporations; industries like electronics, IT, the diamond industry, handicraft and readymade garments—all this in an atmosphere that is pollution-free. It will be a green city providing international standard infrastructure and facilities, including a convention centre and exhibition grounds.

New town planning ought to be eco-friendly and in tune with nature—all sewage water being treated and recycled, additional sewage treatment plants being constructed and garbage being used to produce fuel, gas, electricity, fuel pellets and vermi-compost/organic fertiliser. No sewage water should be disposed in the sea and no garbage should be dumped anywhere. If all this sounds like an impossible dream, well, so did the Mumbai-Pune Expressway not so long ago!

ISN'T NAVI MUMBAI ENOUGH?

The sceptic would ask—but surely we already have one alternative to Mumbai and its success has been uneven. After all, Navi Mumbai itself has taken a long time to thrive.

Well, the fact is, Navi Mumbai is growing faster than one might recognise. In 2001, the city had a population of roughly 750,000 of which approximately 116,842 lived in Nerul and about 111,600 in Vashi, with the remainder residing in Belapur, Kharghar, Sanpada, Airoli, Ghansoli, Kopar Khairane and surrounding areas. This is a gargantuan increase from the official Navi Mumbai Municipal Corporation (NMMC) statistics of 1991, which reported a population of nearly 397,000. The overall increase in population during 1991-2001 itself was 82 per cent. While there are still pockets in the twin cities that have a thin population, they will be filled up quickly, once the new airport comes up.

It is never too early to plan for the future. Navi Mumbai took more than twenty-five years to take shape, from the concept stage to reality. It was as far back as 1948, in the first post-Independence development plan for Mumbai, formulated by the Mayer-Modak Committee, that satellite towns north of the city were suggested. Ten years later, the Barve Committee suggested the formation of a township on the mainland across the Thane Creek. After that, it was only in 1973, that the first concrete steps were taken towards drawing people away from the island city of Mumbai, to the new 344 sq km self-contained metro city that would soon become the Mumbai-Pune Knowledge Corridor. That was the year that the Thane Creek Bridge was opened. It proved to be a lifeline for the developing city. Navi Mumbai is already well on its way to reaching its full potential. But will it be enough for your children, and theirs?

A Third Mumbai could offer several new opportunities, both in terms of industrial development and in terms of decongesting the city. It can offer new avenues for enhanced tourism, entertainment, amusement, hospitality and healthcare industries. Huge amusement and theme parks could be developed near Panvel on the Mumbai-Pune Expressway on the lines of Disneyland or Sentosa. Entertainment centres like Las Vegas, replete with food plazas, exhibition grounds and halls could be set up to attract tourists. The existing Film City could be revitalised with private participation.

A new race course could be developed in the Third Mumbai with breeding and medical centres for horses, better stables and providing world-class facilities for jockeys' training to attract international players. Plus, the Mahalaxmi Race Course could be relocated and the old race course area—once considered the outer limit of the city—could be exploited for commercial use. Facilities for water sports, adventure games, marine exhibitions, a walkthrough aquarium and even a fisherman's village could be developed on a BOT basis in order to attract foreign tourists. A Third Mumbai would help develop tourist potential in more than one way; the Mahananda and Aarey dairies could be relocated here, and the entire Goregaon dairy area could be developed as an eco-friendly tourist destination.

A Third Mumbai would also cater to the growing demands of the entertainment industry. The city can comprise modern studios providing digitised editing facilities, production sets for TV serials, centres for special visual effects, graphics and animation. A major international healthcare centre can also come up in this new city offering all surgical, transplantation and medical research facilities, including organ banks.

As for the traditional wealth of the region, how can one forget the fisher-folk? A Third Mumbai would offer a new lease of life to the fisheries through the creation of modern methods of fishing, storage, processing, packaging and marketing. Surely there is room here even for a seafood plaza!

The Original City Cannot be Ignored

The question that some people will ask is—where does it end? If and when this Third Mumbai does take shape, what will happen once this gets too crowded as well? Will we have to go on to a fourth Mumbai, a fifth, a sixth? The fact is, we have reached a point now when we need to start thinking of a Third Mumbai. This does not, however, mean that the existing cities of Mumbai and Navi Mumbai should be neglected. Permanent solutions can only be found if the problems are attacked from all sides, if a multi-pronged strategy is used and care taken to not allow Mumbai to deteriorate further.

Most importantly, steps ought to be taken to address the vast influx into Mumbai. Estimated to have a floating population of 20 lakh, the city finds it difficult to sustain it.

Migration to bigger cities is not a problem with Mumbai alone. All major Indian cities are facing this problem. The only reason why it is tougher for Mumbai is because of its limited scope for land expansion, considering it is surrounded by water on three sides. A constructive, national approach is required to look into the problem. People will only return to their villages if there is something to go back for. Hence, urgent measures must be taken to improve irrigation facilities for the parched land and create more employment opportunities away from the commercial capital.

A related problem is that of slums. It has often been pointed out that more than half the population of the city lives in slums. Some attempts have been made to rehabilitate slum dwellers but the progress so far has been painfully slow. Yet, this is a concern that can and must be tackled and, as has been proved in Indore, it is not impossible.

In 1989, a civil engineer and planner, Himanshu Parikh, won the Aga Khan Award for Architecture, for his work on the Slum Networking Project in the city of Indore. The city, a distribution centre for agricultural products as well as a source of textile manufacturing, was experiencing a business growth which resulted in an influx of inhabitants drawn to the employment opportunities. Most of these newcomers moved into slums, and an inadequate sewage system soon resulted in waste being deposited into nearby rivers, creating unsanitary conditions.

Parikh, who treated the slums as an integrated part of the city, upgraded the sewage system and involved the slum dwellers in the improvement of their own areas. These areas that were once covered in mud became clean and sanitary. Local residents also took enthusiastic interest in the beautification of the filthy waterfront area where the two regional rivers met.

According to experts in the field of architecture, 'Because of the sensitivity to the needs of the slum inhabitants and an interest in long-term, meaningful improvements to their living conditions, the Slum Networking Project is an uncommon success to a very common Third World problem.'

Rehabilitation of slum dwellers into pucca and hygienic houses is a priority. Viable packages must be created for the developers for sector-wise development of slums and houses must be provided to slum dwellers at concessional and affordable rates and low interest loans. If smaller slums are relocated, the space vacated can be used for residential and commercial purposes.

Khar land (wasteland) could be used for rehabilitation of slums. This rehabilitation should be complete with all amenities and facilities. New gardens and a green belt for the city can be developed on these wastelands. Part of the land can, in addition, be used for construction of large office buildings and parking areas and some South Mumbai offices can be relocated in these buildings, thus de-congesting the area.

All Coastal Regulation Zone (CRZ) areas, beaches and spaces near railway tracks should be freed from encroachments and beautified. Eminent environmentalists and architects must be consulted in designing new town layouts. Open spaces, playgrounds and roads must be protected from encroachments and trees should be planted on their boundaries. *Koliwada*s, the homes of the original inhabitants of Mumbai, should be developed as tourist locations, keeping their ethnic flavour intact.

Another matter which requires great attention is the presence of hawkers in the city. While these hawkers and other small vendors are an essential part of a Mumbaikar's life, their haphazard presence creates major traffic jams and public nuisance. Special authorised markets for vegetables, fruits, flowers, fish and mutton must be created and hawkers' plazas should be set up wherever possible.

Hawkers, of course, are not the only cause of traffic jams. The fundamental issue here is the increasing number of vehicles on roads which were simply not designed to carry such a volume of traffic. The government should adopt strong steps to restrict the number of vehicles in the city. One of the possible ways could be to not allow a vehicle to be purchased until the buyer can show he has a permanent parking space. The other potent way is to make public transport comfortable enough for people to sacrifice the luxury of their own vehicles.

Water scarcity is another major problem that plagues Mumbai, especially in those years when rainfall is below normal. I have dwelt upon this problem in greater detail in the chapter on natural resource management.

There is much that remains to be done in Mumbai—development rules need to be followed strictly in all construction activities, and the people themselves, the inhabitants of this amazing city, must take a keener interest in rejuvenating it. Planners and policy makers can only provide the framework, but this city, which belongs to you and to me, is crying for attention.

Extrapolating Mumbai's Challenges to study the Larger Town Planning Scenario in India

With migration from villages to cities being a uniform pattern across the country, several Indian cities and towns have grown exponentially in the last few decades. Like Mumbai, the existing infrastructure of these cities stands burdened and, in many cases, is on the verge of collapse. This only reiterates the importance of planning our cities for the future.

Interestingly, archaeological evidence corroborates ancient India's brilliance in the field of town planning. The impeccable planning of Harappa and Mohenjo-Daro surprises us even today. Post-Independence, we have created some excellent towns like Gandhinagar, Chandigarh and Bhubaneswar. However, these cities stand in isolation even as conditions in most other places continue to deteriorate rapidly.

Since we missed the bus in 1947, the least we can do now to control the damage is to identify fifteen of the worst cities in terms of traffic congestion, pollution, water scarcity, drainage systems, etc. Over a period of ten to fifteen years, the idea should be to address the problems of these cities. Planning an extended twin city is thus a viable option towards easing the pressures on the existing city infrastructure.

One example of this, which instantly comes to my mind, is New Raipur, the new capital of Chhattisgarh which has been, and is still being, built 17 km away in the south-east direction from the existing capital city, Raipur. Interestingly, the new city includes forty-one villages out of which twenty-seven form the core of New Raipur. It is always a huge challenge to plan a new township with minimal displacement of existing population or the best possible rehabilitation for them. New Raipur comes out with flying colours in this aspect.

Here, I would like to make a special mention of the proposed coastal city of Dholera in Gujarat. Set up on the Delhi Mumbai Industrial Corridor, the proposed city is very strategically located at a distance of 110 km from Ahmedabad and 132 km form Vadodara. It is my firm belief that, when this city becomes functional by 2018, it will not just decongest Ahmedabad and Vadodara, but create new business opportunities for businessmen from Mumbai as well.

However, there are cities which do not have much room for expansion, such as Patna, Lucknow or Kanpur. The task of exploring alternative transport and setting up a water reusage mechanism needs to be expedited in these cities.

At the same time, the viability of water transport needs to be explored wherever possible. Recently, a senior party leader from Madhya Pradesh shared with me a proposal he had for metro rail connectivity in Bhopal. I, instead, asked him to explore a far more cost-effective alternative. Bhopal is a city of lakes. I asked him to draw up a proposal that would connect all these lakes with each other. In that situation, like metro stations in Delhi, we could have boat stations in different parts of the city and boats could ferry people from one place to the other. This would also help explore the tourism potential of Bhopal, which is one of the most beautiful cities in India.

One needs to understand that the challenges today are very different from those that existed two or three decades ago. The housing boom has changed the scenario in urban areas. New localities have sprung up, away from the main towns and cities. As a result, the highways have shrunk and towns have come up along these. One example of this is the proposed Delhi-Mumbai Industrial Corridor. The corridor envisages the creation of ten cities along its route. In my opinion, it is an excellent example of employment-aided decongestion of important cities. Of course, the new cities need to be planned in an environment-friendly way.

A comprehensive plan of action needs to be drawn up in so far as town planning for the future is concerned. For this, the Urban Development Ministry should draw up a concrete vision plan. What is equally important is effective coordination with the state governments and local self-governing bodies to ensure that these efforts bear fruit.

Nagpur: A City of Untapped Potential

The city where you are born and bred always holds a special place in your heart. It is the same for me too. Nagpur holds a special place in my heart and I have always tried to do my extra bit to ensure that the city gets the best.

It is the largest city in central India and the third largest city by population in Maharashtra. It has a population of around 2.4 million people. The British East India Company took over Nagpur in the nineteenth century and made it the capital of the Central Provinces and Berar. After the first reorganisation of states, the city lost its capital status but according to the informal 'Nagpur Pact' between political leaders, it was made the second capital of Maharashtra. Interestingly, Nagpur lies precisely at the centre of the country with the Zero Mile Marker indicating the geographical centre of India.

Personally, there are many fond memories which I associate with this city—some happy and some not too pleasant. These myriad memories of my life in this city remain with me wherever I go: The difficult times my family faced when I was young; the inspiration that the poetry of Sant Tukaram gave me; my college years when I was quite certain that I will be a lawyer; the elocution competitions which invariably fetched me rich rewards, including a university gold medal.

There are also memories of hardships which, when I look back now, I can have a good laugh at. Once, when I lost in the university elections by a narrow margin, I took out a celebratory procession, much like a winner would. People found it strange. But there was a philosophy for it—to enjoy life every moment and not allow your setbacks to get the better of you. In fact, one should have the ability to laugh at one's failures.

I feel God has given me a lot, more than what I had imagined. And through my success and failure, if there has been a constant companion, it has been the city of Nagpur—its roads, its alleys and its walls. Throughout my growing up years, what upset me the most was that even after years and decades of change, the progress of Nagpur was extremely tardy. I was a witness to the infrastructure of Nagpur deteriorating due to governmental neglect. Being the only city in a vastly under-developed region, it attracted migrants in huge numbers from the neighbouring villages. The existing roads, thus, became narrow and congested; the city became dirty and electricity and water supply were hit as well. Nagpur, due to its multiple problems, resembled an overgrown village.

So, in 1995, when I became the PWD minister and the

guardian minister in the then Maharashtra government, I knew it was time for me to give something back to the city to which I owed so much.

My first task after becoming guardian minister was to set aside ₹20 crore annually for the various development initiatives in the city. The Nagpur Improvement Trust (NIT) and the Nagpur Municipal Corporation (NMC) were required to pool in an equal sum for the purpose. Raising ₹40 crore a year, thus meant raising ₹200 crore in five years. This amount was spent on giving Nagpur the makeover it long needed.

In the Nagpur region, around 200 km of roads belonged to the PWD ministry. I ensured that this stretch got funds speedily from my department and on a priority basis. Other than this, I introduced a comprehensive road development programme for the city called the Integrated Road Development Program (IRDP). The total money allotted under this scheme was ₹335 crore.

Similarly, I raised money through some other sources also. At the end of my tenure as minister—nearly ₹1,000 crore had been spent on the improvement of Nagpur. Our major initiatives involved widening of roads, construction of cement roads for the first time in the city, various beautification initiatives and also constructing Nagpur's first flyover. At that time, my decision to introduce a flyover drew a lot of criticism. Today, it is universally accepted that, had the flyover not been constructed, the traffic situation would have been pathetic.

I wish to acknowledge here, the special role played by the NMC and NIT in improving the living conditions in the city. In fact, we tend to underestimate the role of local self-governing bodies. But in my opinion, the role these civic bodies have to play is unparalleled.

I have been one of the strongest votaries for empowering local self-governing bodies in order to effectively address local issues. Besides, they need the support and guidance of state and national-level politicians in optimising their true potential. With this view in mind, I have always taken active interest in the functioning of the NMC, giving them suggestions and making myself available whenever they need my inputs.

The biggest problem that municipal corporations face is paucity of funds. Often, they have great ideas of improving the sanitation facilities or beautifying a city. But many a times they are held back because the funds at their disposal are terribly inadequate. Hence, my focus has always been on how to make these organisations financially self-sufficient.

My request to all the mayors in various municipal corporations is that they should dream big. They should dream to make their city the best and a model city. I assure you that you can create magic by doing so. It is not at all difficult. And it does not even require much money. It only requires a vision and a will to work. With a willingness to exchange ideas and share information, we can attain huge results. There is a latent talent in all of us, we need to tap it and use it to change our environment, our society and our country.

Let me share my little experience of how we handled the civic development programmes in Nagpur.

MIHAN

While improvement of roads and infrastructure is a very basic developmental need, we required a broader vision to create an apparatus that would sustain the development of Nagpur. That could not happen unless viable employment opportunities were generated in the region. The city was entitled to its due, regardless of who was its guardian minister and which government ruled the state.

What the region needed, thus, was an economic apparatus that would create multiple avenues for commerce and employment. The quest for this all-encompassing apparatus is what led me to conceive a plan called Multi-modal International Cargo Hub and Airport at Nagpur (MIHAN).

I will briefly explain what MIHAN[1] is. It is the biggest economic development project currently underway in India in terms of investment. It is spread over an area of 4,354 hectares in and around Nagpur.

The project consists of two parts, an international airport to act as a cargo hub and an SEZ with residential zone, covering a total area of 40.25 sq km on the southern end of Nagpur. The estimated capital cost of the project is ₹2,581 crore (by the year 2035) and is supposed to generate revenues worth ₹5,280 crore.

The project has several constituent objectives: First, to meet the demands of increasing air traffic in India and provide the required world-class infrastructure for the aviation sector, the existing airport of 400 hectares would be expanded to 1,364 hectares. The airport will have parking space for fifty aircrafts at any time with fifty additional bays at fringe area.

Secondly, a new SEZ of 2,086 hectares, the largest multi-product SEZ in India, would be built alongside the airport. Out of 2,086 hectares, 1,472 hectares would be used by various processing units to be set up and the remaining 614 hectares would be for service sector units. Like all SEZs, it will have financial incentives and soft taxation policy to attract investment. The initial set-up material for these units and later raw material will be duty-free.

Major sections of the SEZ will comprise an IT park, spread over 500 hectares and would include all necessary infrastructure for IT companies, a health city spread over 40 hectares that will have multi-specialty hospitals, manufacturing industry unit that would include industries from sectors like textile and garment, gems and jewellery, food processing, pharmaceuticals and biomedical. It would also have units for finance and insurance service companies.

Several other infrastructural requirements are taken care of in the proposal in such a way that the project would meet the highest standards of sustainable, economically efficient town planning.

It is important to understand here why Nagpur is best suited for a project like MIHAN. Our two biggest airports, Delhi and Mumbai, are over-used and congested. Besides, as Delhi is in the north and Mumbai at one western end, the cost of transporting the cargo from these two airports to their actual destination is quite high. Nagpur, with its most central location and unused space, fits the bill better. Therefore, it makes logical sense to have all cargo landing activities shifted to this particular destination. While all cargo flights flying from the east and Southeast Asia will save on their fuel cost, the transport costs of distributing this cargo within our country will also reduce.

Besides, Vidarbha being an under-developed region, the project can permanently address its unemployment problem. It can partially help in controlling the rising number of suicides by farmers of the area as well.

Lastly, as I have always maintained, we must look at those broader initiatives that would decongest our cities and make people shift to smaller towns. For equitable distribution of wealth between different regions, we must also attempt equitable distribution of skilled professionals. MIHAN, with its huge employment potential, will have abundant opportunities to draw our best professionals from the bigger cities.

In all these years, from the time the project was first conceived, I have pursued it passionately. In fact, I have organised and spoken at rallies that were solely meant to mobilise public support for the MIHAN project. Similarly, I have travelled to other districts of Vidarbha to try and educate the masses about the vast usefulness of this project.

However, I have to say this with regret that the Maharashtra government has shown very little urgency in completing the project. The MIHAN project, just like the Mumbai-Pune Expressway, requires greater political backing, which unfortunately the Maharashtra government has not been able to provide.

Thinking is progress. Non-thinking is stagnation of the individual, organisation and the country. Thinking leads to action. Knowledge without action is useless and irrelevant. Knowledge with action converts adversity into prosperity.

— APJ Abdul Kalam

SIX

Natural Resource Management

Natural resource management, a much used term today, refers to the management of natural resources such as land, water, soil, plants and animals with a particular focus on how their management affects the quality of life for both present and future generations.

Unlike man-made resources, natural resources cannot be expanded at will. However, the phenomenal rate at which our population has grown in the last century has imposed severe demands on the availability of these natural resources. The mismanagement or absence of planning, including the lack of adequate irrigation facilities, has led to poor agricultural growth. Vast areas of our country grapple with an acute deficit of clean drinking water, causing high infant mortality, besides leading to the spread of waterborne diseases. The drought and flood situations have only been aggravated due to our inability to manage the water resources. On the other hand, lack of initiatives for reusing water has made us lose out on opportunities for industrial growth and electricity generation. Similarly, huge stretches of land in our country rot as wasteland. Sadly, we have no concrete plan in place to reclaim and utilise this wasteland.

Today, approximately 15 per cent of our population does not have access to clean drinking water. Similarly, more than 40 per cent of the farmers do not have access to proper irrigation facilities. The situation makes it imperative for us to draw out a clear strategy to manage these resources to ensure that our future generations are not left battling an even worse situation of want. And for this, we need a futuristic approach. For instance, when addressing the problem of water management, one has to forecast the challenges that we would be facing fifteen or twenty years from now. It will be of no use if we draw up plans based on present-day estimates. For, by the time we will be ready to implement these, the demands would have grown, making our solutions unfeasible. When talking about water management, one area which has been of keen interest to me is optimising reuse of water. Reused water can be used for almost all purposes other than drinking. In all my growing up years, Nagpur has grappled with acute shortage of water. In those days, technology was not available. But in the present age of globalisation, it is easy to install a mechanism for purifying used water and enabling its reuse. All it takes is the will to make it happen.

I wish to acquaint you with the commendable work done by NMC with its path-breaking initiatives in this direction.

Institutionalising Reuse of Water

Since I have spent all my life in Vidarbha, an under-developed region, most of my thoughts have emerged from the desire to improve the pathetic conditions in the area. Scarcity of water is the biggest concern in the area, as also an important cause of other major problems. It adversely affects electricity production which, in turn, inhibits industrial growth, letting the entire region remain a backward zone.

As I have mentioned, I tried to do my bit towards addressing the problem with the initiatives of the Purti Group. However, what the region needs is more such initiatives. To address the problem of unemployment, Vidarbha needs industrial growth. And industrial growth is impossible without adequate supply of water. Water is a limited resource. As the population of Nagpur has grown rapidly in the last few decades, we needed an innovative plan to ensure that water was available for the city's growing needs.

I have travelled to various countries with the objective of studying how they have adapted themselves to new challenges of development amid increased scarcities. If there is something that has impressed me the most, it is how leading countries of the world have set a mechanism in place for water reusage.

'Reuse' of water is a constant process that goes on in nature. Considering nature to be our teacher, we must adopt the same process. The increase in population results in setting up of new industries, hence, the demand for water grows as well. This is the main road towards development and to make this road more capacious, reuse of water is the most plausible solution.

I was, thus, convinced that Nagpur needed its own water reuse mechanism. When I am convinced that something ought to be done, my determination finds ways to do it. Running to the state government for every problem is often not the solution. Instead, if the municipal corporation in every city takes up such issues aggressively, it sometimes eases the pressure on the state government.

I have always believed that local self-governments

need encouragement from state and national-level leaders, as they have a huge potential to deliver. And this was proved in the way the NMC planned the execution of the path-breaking water reuse project in the city. In 2008, the NMC struck a deal with the Maharashtra State Power Generation Company Limited (Mahagenco). According to the deal, NMC agreed to supply 110 Million Litres per Day (MLD) treated wastewater to Mahagenco, to be utilised for power generation in the latter's Khaperkheda and Koradi thermal power plants. In return, Mahagenco approved an annual payment of ₹15 crore to the NMC for a thirty-year period. This amount provided the fund for the future development initiatives of the corporation and led to the improvement of the city.

This financial model of recycling sewage water and selling it to meet the surplus demands of the industry was a first of its kind step for an Indian municipal corporation. If the scientific processes of purification and disinfection are applied, the reused water can be used for all requirements except for drinking. Of course, the conversion of sewage into its reusable form will require setting up the necessary processes, which cannot happen overnight. This is a result of continuous effort.

The city of Nagpur has gained in many ways from this project, the main advantage being that 110 MLD of pure water can be conserved, thereby solving the water problem of nearly 800,000 people. The population of Nagpur is 2.4 million, according to Census 2011. The city gets its water supply from natural resources like Kanhan and Pench rivers. Lake Gorewada is also used as a water reservoir within the city periphery. Together, these resources supply approximately 470 MLD of water to the city. Out of this, 80 per cent of the total water supply gets converted into sewage. According to a sewage treatment project, Malnisaran, the city is divided into three parts, North,

Central and South Nagpur. Each region produces nearly 100, 180 and 100 lakh litre of sewage every day respectively. These figures reinforce the fact that utilising the sewage can provide a permanent solution to the problem of water scarcity in the city.

The demand for water supply and the sewage treatment by 2031				
S. No.	Year	Population (million)	Water Supply (MLD)	Sewage (MLD)
1.	2005	2.35	470	380
2.	2011	2.83	532	426
3.	2021	3.69	709	567
4.	2031	4.75	934	747

From this chart we come to know that, in the coming years, there will be a great need of large underground sewage canals and dirt removal centres in Nagpur city.[1]

The reason why I wanted to share this initiative of the NMC is essentially because it is a path-breaking leadership initiative that must be emulated everywhere, in as many Indian cities and towns as possible. It is not always necessary that the Central or state government shows us the way. On the contrary, the NMC has shown the way to the state government to formulate its own policies in this direction.

I would take this example to reiterate the importance of effective local self-governing bodies. Two aspects of the working of a local self-government have been of keen interest to me. Can these bodies become financially self-sufficient? Can they take the lead in environmental protection? The historic NMC programme, which institutionalises reuse of water, has given me answers to both these questions.

There is tremendous scope to generate revenue from

sources that we have been ignorant of. All it requires is an entrepreneurial bent of mind to gauge such opportunities. Besides its known advantages, reuse of water also helps the environment in a significant way. It brings down the need to divert water from sensitive ecosystems. Other benefits include decreasing wastewater discharges and reducing and preventing pollution. Recycled water can also be used to create or improve wetlands and riparian habitats.

River-linking

One of the reasons why water availability and management continues to be such an uphill task in India is due to an escapist attitude towards it by the Central government. What augments the problem is the diverse nature of difficulties faced by our country. Climatic changes differ significantly from one part of the country to the other. Every year, some parts of India grapple with drought while others negotiate the fury of floods. By reducing the river flow to the oceans and diverting the surplus water to areas where there is water shortage, we can address these problems.

I am saddened to note the vast damage that has occurred in recent years due to overflowing rivers and incessant rains in the country. This has not only caused a large number of deaths but has also left tens of thousands of people marooned and forced a similar number to become homeless. In Delhi alone, in 2010, even as the city was preparing to host the Commonwealth Games, a significant population was affected by the unprecedented flooding of the Yamuna river, unheard of in the last three decades. Other states like Uttar Pradesh, Bihar, Odisha and Uttarakhand have been hit by heavy floods in recent years, resulting in huge losses of life and property.

While all the relief measures of the Central and state governments—starting from minimising the casualties, to rehabilitation of affected people and rebuilding the roads and other infrastructure etc.—kick off post the disaster, what we need to look into is whether there is anything that can be done in order to minimise such damage. While we cannot regulate rainfall and its effects in terms of flooding, what we can certainly do is minimise the impact of floods. Interlinking of rivers in the country can address these problems.

When the excess rainwater in a river basin cannot be stored in reservoirs built on that river, it inundates the surrounding places. While it is common to build large dams and reservoirs to store river water, it is uncommon to plan and build major dams and reservoirs for storing floodwater. That is where the benefit of interlinking of rivers comes into the picture. When excess rainfall is recorded in a given river basin and if there is no way of controlling the floodwater in the already existing reservoirs on that river, instead of letting that water run downstream and inundate the surroundings, if we could transfer that water to a water-deficit river basin, then we would be able to reduce the submergence downstream. This would not only reduce the impact and damage caused by the floods but would also transfer the excess water to another water-deficit river basin which can benefit the inhabitants of that region.

In the year 2010, about 3,500 Thousand Million Cubic feet (TMC) of water went waste into the sea from Godavari, Krishna and Vamsadhara rivers in South India due to excessive rainfall during the monsoon. If this water had been transferred and stored in reservoirs in water deficit regions, then the farmers in the southern states would have benefitted a lot. With the help of this stored water, they would have been able to raise crops in the rabi season, when rainwater is a scarcity. Most of the rivers in South India flow actively during the months of June and September, for a period of two to three months.

During monsoon, these rivers swell, causing floods and severe damage. All these problems can be solved if earnest steps are taken to interlink Mahanadi with Godavari. Due to this interlinking of rivers, the South India water grid will get connected to the north India water grid, thus forming an All-India Water Grid.

I wish to share with you an excellent example of river connectivity. The state of Gujarat has effectively undertaken interlinking of rivers to divert water from surplus to deficit river basins. The successfully completed projects include the Harnav to Guhai Link and the Sabarmati to Saraswati Link, both in the state of Gujarat. The excess waters of Narmada and Mahi rivers are channelled through the Narmada main canal. Escapes are provided into seventeen en route rivers on the alignment of the Narmada main canal that include Mazam, Meshvo, Khari, Sabarmati, Pushpavati, Saraswati, Banas rivers, thus interlinking Narmada and Mahi with these rivers. Apart from the escapes provided, to directly pour the water from the canal to these rivers, water is lifted through pipelines from this canal to extreme end reservoirs of these rivers in east Gujarat so that the rivers are charged at these points itself while flowing towards west Gujarat. The Narmada main canal is also linked to the other river basins in the water scarcity regions of Saurashtra and Kutch through gravity canals.

In fact, one of the most revolutionary initiatives in river-linking was undertaken by the Gujarat government in the year 2004. The Sujalam Suphlam Yojana, as it was called, provided an integrated approach to augment water resources in water deficit and over-exploited areas. Under this programme, a 332 km long canal was built, crossing 21 rivers on its route. Fourteen lift irrigation pipelines were built to fill nine reservoirs and ponds of north Gujarat. This has not only provided irrigation facilities but also drinking water supply to all the villages and towns. In addition to this, Gujarat has built 130,000 check-dams that act as a means for groundwater recharge. So, the water that is transferred across the river basins is appropriately used in these check-dams to regenerate groundwater that rejuvenate rivers that have gone dry.

In 2003, when the NDA government was in power, the National Water Development Agency (NWDA) had divided the interlinking of rivers into three major components—the intra-state links, the peninsular component and the Himalayan part. The project proposed to link fourteen Himalayan rivers in the north and sixteen peninsular rivers in the south. The initial projected cost of the programme was ₹560,000 crore. In 2003-04, our government at the Centre was determined to embark upon the project with a targeted completion date of 2016. However, in 2004, after the UPA came to power, this project, like several other development projects, was put on the backburner. In 2009, it was called off altogether.

As it has happened before in our country, even before the project could take off, there were pessimists who started pointing out its flaws. There are broadly three points of contention: One, the total estimated cost of the project and whether such investment would yield productive results; two, its potential harmful impact on the environment; three, the problem of displacement of the population.

Every historical move is fraught with risks and uncertainties. Does that mean we abandon them? As an optimist, I am confident that we can find solutions to all these concerns. Given the benefits of the project, which will accrue over several hundred years, I am convinced that this is an opportunity we cannot afford to lose out on. In fact, we stand committed to revive the project when we form the government at the Centre.

I am happy to note that in recent years, certain

developments have taken place independently in the direction of river-linking. The Somasila project in South India was completed before schedule as it had the support of religious leaders who vouched for its usefulness to the people. Similarly, the support of locals ensured that the Jalgaon project in Maharashtra, where Girna and Bori rivers were interlinked, was completed within six months. Hence, there are ways in which support, either from religious leaders or local panchayats, can remove perceived impediments.

Then in May 2010, with an aim to provide water to arid and water deficit areas, Gujarat and Maharashtra signed a pact with the Central government to prepare project reports to inter-link several rivers in their region. The tripartite MOU was signed by the chief ministers of Gujarat and Maharashtra and the Union Water Resources Minister in the presence of the Prime Minister.

The proposed Damanganga-Pinjal and Par-Tapi-Narmada links are two inter-basin water transfer links concerning Gujarat and Maharashtra. While the Damanganga-Pinjal link mainly benefits Maharashtra, the Par-Tapi-Narmada link would mainly benefit regions in Gujarat. This link will transfer surplus water available between Rivers Par and Tapi in Gujarat to the deficit areas of north Gujarat. It will transfer 1,350 million cubic metres through a 402 km long gravity canal. The total en route irrigation benefits envisaged are 1.88 lakh hectares in Gujarat. Besides, there is also a provision of generating 32.5 MW of electricity. Maharashtra will benefit from the Damanganga-Pinjal link through augmentation of water supply for Mumbai city. The state government in Gujarat would be entitled to utilise the remaining spillover waters from the Bhugal and Khargihill dams in this link.

I would hail this as a historical step in the direction of re-initiating the national river-linking project. These independent developments only reiterate the importance of linking up all our waterbodies. If the same is carried out across the country in a planned manner, most of the problems of rural and urban India will be solved.

I wish to point out a few things here.

One, while I have the highest regard for the environment, there is something wrong with the approach of a section of Indian environmental activists. River-linking has been successfully executed in several countries of the world. In India, given our deficits, its urgency increases. We must all sit together and identify the environmental dangers, if any. But our approach should be one of finding solutions and not one of stalling things.

Two, in India, state governments have been locked in water disputes among themselves. Therefore, it is not unnatural for some governments to have apprehensions that other states might benefit more from their resources. Such apprehensions must be allayed. The basic idea of the river-linking project is to correct inequalities. Moreover, the governments should think from a holistic perspective and put the nation's interests first.

Three, a massive rehabilitation plan needs to be put in place for the families that are likely to be displaced by this project.

In the earlier chapters, I have emphasised enough on the difference that water makes to a village. I am sure the river-linking project is a historical opportunity to revive our golden era.

Water Desalination

India has a coastline of 7,600 km, spreading over 10 states. What is surprising is the acute water shortage even in the coastal regions. This is where the process of desalination of water can come in handy.

Desalination refers to any of several processes that remove some amount of salt and other minerals from water.

More generally, desalination is also used in reference to the removal of salts and minerals as in soil desalination, making the agricultural land in coastal areas more conducive to farming. This technology has been used in many parts of the world, including the USA, Saudi Arabia, Israel and even the Maldives, with success. In India, considering our vast coastline, it is surprising that we did not consider this option seriously until recently.

However, in the last few years, some work has been carried out in this direction.

The world's first ever Low Temperature Thermal Desalination plant (LTTD) was set up in Kavaratti, the capital of Lakshadweep, in May 2005. The plant cost about ₹50 million and produces 100,000 litres of potable water per day from seawater. Nine sites were identified in Lakshadweep for setting up of desalination plants by the National Institute of Ocean Technology (NIOT). Three more LTTD desalination plants, one each in Agatti, Minicoy and Andrott, have also been set up in 2012. Work on the remaining five islands—Chetlat, Kadmat, Kiltan, Kalpeni and Amini will be taken up after successful commissioning of the first set of three plants through the PPP model. The production capacity of freshwater for each of the proposed plant is 100,000 litre per day.

In August 2010, India's largest desalination plant was inaugurated near Chennai. The facility draws water from the Bay of Bengal, processes it using the reverse osmosis technology, and supplies purified water to the city. The ₹600-crore plant at Minjur, 35 km north of Chennai, is the state's first water desalination plant. Set up as a joint venture between IVRCL Infrastructures Ltd and Befesa, a globally renowned company specialising in generation and management of water, the plant can process and supply 100 million litres of water per day. This amount is expected to meet the needs of 2 million people. The plant supplies water to Chennai Metropolitan Water Supply at a cost of ₹48.74 per 1,000 litres and is committed to do so for 25 years.

Mumbai, which faces the stiffest infrastructural challenges, was late in waking up to this technology. I had proposed this method way back in 1998-99 when the BJP-Shiv Sena government ruled Maharashtra. The successive governments did not even consider it seriously.

But I am glad that at present, the Mumbai Metropolitan Region Development Authority (MMRDA) is planning to set up desalination plants in the Vasai-Virar Municipal Corporation belt, the Mira-Bhayandar Municipal Corporation belt and one in the main city. The MMRDA proposes to produce 500 million litres of potable water every day through these plants. These plans are, however, at a nascent stage and it will take time before Mumbai's water woes are wished away. The city's erratic monsoon in the last few years, along with steep growth in population, makes it an imperative to make these desalination plants operative at the earliest. It surprises me that such initiatives were not considered seriously until now.

Given India's vast coastline, water desalination lends itself naturally as a solution to our water problems, especially in coastal areas. It will definitely incur a higher cost than some of the other alternatives. But given its potential, we must work towards setting viable financial plans in place to enable more and more parts of the country to benefit from this technology.

Wasteland Management

Wasteland management is another area of keen interest for me. As I have mentioned, I am reminded of the gravity of the problem every time I fly from one part of the country to the other. Right across the country, one can spot such huge bodies of unused wasteland that it leaves you wondering why no systematic efforts have been made to reclaim these lands. Even if a fraction of it is successfully retrieved and put to productive use, it will improve India's national income significantly. India shares approximately 17 per cent of the world population, while her land is only about 2.4 per cent of the total geographical area of the world. This has led to a significant decline in the productivity of our land resources and resultantly, in our national income. To be fair to the government, I must admit some thought has gone into the issue of watershed management. In fact, Rajiv Gandhi had shown interest in this wasteland management. The National Wasteland Development Board was established in 1985 under the Ministry of Forests and Environment, mainly to tackle the problem of degradation of lands, restoration of ecology and to meet the growing demands of fuelwood and fodder at the national level. Subsequently, the Department for Land Resources under the Ministry of Rural Development had constituted an Integrated Wasteland Development Program (IWDP). According to the data available from this department, wastelands constitute a total area of 638,518.31 sq km under various categories.

A break-up of the different categories of wastelands is listed here[2]:

Category	Area (in sq km)	Category	Area (in sq km)	Category	Area (in sq. km)
Snow-covered/ glacier	55,788.49	Water logged and marshy	16,568.45	Gullied/ ravenous land	20,553.35
Barren rocky/ sheet rock	64,584.77	Steep sloping area	7,656.29	Upland with or without scrub	194,014.29
Sands-inland/ coastal	50,021.65	Shifting cultivation land	35,142.2	Degraded/ pastures/ grazing land	25,978.91

Land affected by salinity/ alkalinity	20,477.38	Mining/ industrial wastelands	1,252.13	Underutilised/ degraded notified forest land	140,652.31
				Degraded land under plantation crop	5,828.09
Grand Total: 638,518.31 sq km					

India has a total land area of approximately 3,287,263 sq km, which effectively means that nearly 20 per cent of the country's land resources are wastelands.

In November 1994, the Department of Wastelands Development had constituted a high-level committee under the chairmanship of Mohan Dharia, former deputy chairman, Planning Commission, to review a strategy and plan of action for the development of vast areas of non-forest wastelands. The committee submitted its report to the then Prime Minister, PV Narasimha Rao, in December 1995.

The Mohan Dharia Committee had underscored the need to develop nearly 175 million hectares of degraded wastelands in the country over the next 10 to 15 years. The report also recommended that every state should prepare a ten-fifteen year perspective plan for proper water and land use and wastelands development. The report recommended to bring all afforestation, wastelands development, soil and water conservation and related schemes under a suitably structured and empowered coordinating authority at the Centre and to replicate it at the state, district and panchayat levels. The authority would coordinate linkage of different schemes and see that a common approach to degraded lands and wastelands is adopted.

I hail the Mohan Dharia Committee report as a historic step in this direction. However, the problem in our country is the deficit between a vision and its execution. This country has some exceptional thinkers but we are often let down by our inactive leadership. I am saddened to note that despite Mohan Dharia having shown us the path, not much has been done by the government in the last fifteen years. As a result, the problem of wastelands continues to be as big a problem as it was twenty-five years ago.

Having said this, I am willing to acknowledge the difficulties involved in this task. The cost of reclaiming many of these wastelands is very high. Besides, even after they are reclaimed, it will require a huge investment in order to sustain them as reclaimed lands. However, this excuse cannot cover up our failure to recover even those wastelands which could have been reclaimed without difficulty.

As with other initiatives, we need more sincerity and a systematic approach towards addressing this problem. Excuses there can be aplenty. So are the opportunities. We, as a nation, have to decide whether we must look for opportunities or excuses.

Be a lamp to yourself. Be your own confidence. Hold to the truth within yourself as the only truth.

—Gautam Buddha

SEVEN

Green Energy

Justifying Biofuel

I have been one of the strongest supporters of the use of biofuel in our country. And the reason is simple. In my opinion, biofuel is critical to our economy. I will explain how.

We spend more than a third of our total budgetary spending every year on importing crude oil. Our fuel price, thus, is subject to the vagaries of the international market. Besides, the money spent on importing the oil anyway increases the cost for the end user. As a result, petrol and diesel prices have been increasing regularly in the last few years. After petroleum prices were de-regulated by the government in 2012, the hike in petrol and diesel prices have been rather cruel. Fuel prices have a direct bearing on the prices of almost all commodities. As a result, prices of essential items have also increased by a huge proportion, causing severe hardships to the common man.

It was more than a decade ago that the NDA government held extensive deliberations on the issue. Even then, I had advocated that India adopt biofuel as an official alternative. If Brazil can do this successfully, why can't we?

Besides, using biofuel has several advantages. It reduces the price of fuel and causes less damage to the environment. The biggest advantage of adopting biofuel will go to the farmers. According to the NCRB, the Accidental Deaths and Suicides report, 290,470 farmers have committed suicide in India from 1995-2011. If the farm sector in India can be channelised to produce biofuel, it can partially solve the problem of poverty and unemployment.

I have been continuously lobbying for the use of ethanol (using 10 to 20 per cent of ethanol in petrol and diesel) as a blending ingredient in petroleum fuels. By doing this, we can aim to reduce the large import of petroleum products so that this saves outflow to foreign countries, which will go to Indian farmers, thereby boosting the economy.

Increasing the production of ethanol is very crucial in giving biofuel the required push. Ethanol is made using molasses, which is a by-product of sugarcane. The government must put a proper plan of action in place for biofuel usage so that the sugar factories are given incentives to take up the production of ethanol on a large scale. Depending upon feasibility, these sugar factory owners can venture into producing biofuel as well. Or else, they derive additional business by supplying ethanol to companies producing biofuel.

In Brazil, up to 22 per cent ethanol is mixed in petroleum products to prepare biofuel. If this happens in India, it will enable us to reduce the amount spent on import of crude oil by 22 per cent. If the amount thus saved is diverted to the agricultural sector, one can imagine the gains to our economy. Even if ₹10,000 crore is systematically invested every year into this initiative, it should generate employment for at least 100,000 people.

For this, it is important to work at different levels simultaneously, as the issue also constitutes a matter of tribal welfare. As I have mentioned in a preceding chapter, the tribals in Vidarbha have been selling the seeds of *erandi*, *karanji*, *moha*, *saal* and *ratnajyoti* to the Purti Group. These seeds are processed to make biodiesel. This engagement has resulted in generating employment opportunities and helped in improving the conditions of life for the tribals in the region. There is a need to explore similar opportunities in other tribal belts across the country. In fact, even if the government is found lagging in such efforts, private entrepreneurs must seize the initiative and help the economy of the area grow thus.

I will be failing in my responsibilities if I do not acknowledge the path-breaking initiatives of the Chhattisgarh government towards encouraging biofuel usage. In a massive drive launched in 2006, the Chhattisgarh government created a world record by planting at least 3 million saplings of jatropha and *karanji* in only 11 hours on a single day to raise awareness about the plants that are rich sources of biofuel. In 3 years, the government had planted 100 million saplings.

All major initiatives have been successful because of the participation of top level leaders. Chief Minister Raman Singh has truly led by example. His own official car runs on biofuel since 2005. To my knowledge, all vehicles of the Chhattisgarh government presently run on biofuel.

In fact, with the specific aim of promoting biofuel usage, the state government had set up an organisation called the Chhattisgarh Biofuel Development Authority (CBDA) in 2005, following the report of the National Mission on Biodiesel submitted by the Planning Commission, Government of India, in the year 2003. The state government further formulated an exhaustive programme for producing biodiesel in substantial quantities over the next seven to eight years.

According to the projections made, this programme can lead to massive socio-economic benefits for the state of Chhattisgarh and make it biofuel self reliant by 2015:

- As 1 hectare of jatropha plantation yields 2 tonnes of biodiesel on an average, total quantity of 20 lakh tonnes of biodiesel will be produced valued at ₹9,400 crore (at ₹47 per litre).
- In undertaking jatropha plantation on 10 lakh hectares of fallow land, manual labour to the tune of almost 30 crore man-days would be required for digging the pits, planting the saplings, inter-culture operations and other agricultural operations for the first two years. Financially, this will translate into ₹1,800 crore as per current agriculture labour wages.
- The proposed large-scale jatropha plantation will substantially reduce greenhouse gases in the atmosphere by absorbing CO_2 which can be traded internationally to the countries having higher pollution levels, in the light of Kyoto protocol.
- By processing jatropha crops worth 1 million hectares, apart from getting 20 lakh tonnes of biodiesel, 40 lakh tonnes of premium quality of bio manure would be produced for use in agriculture sector. This bio manure (6%N), besides providing much needed micro nutrients to the soil, will also help in preserving humus which is getting unbalanced due to the persistent and uncontrolled use of chemical fertilisers. Even by taking a nominal cost of ₹8 per kg for this bio manure, the

total value of the bio manure so produced will be in the region of ₹3200 crore annually.[1]

Thus, the benefits of using biofuel are too vast and diversified to be squandered away. Chhattisgarh, with its path-breaking initiatives, has set an example for the entire country.

I want to go a step further here. Can we try and develop engines that run entirely on ethanol?

Several countries have successfully experimented with ethanol engines. Flex fuel, or E85, is a mixture of up to 85 per cent denatured fuel ethanol and gasoline or other hydrocarbon (HC) by volume. On the other hand, some vehicles such as the Ford Model T can operate on 100 per cent pure alcohol fuel. However, it is more common to combine gasoline and ethanol to receive some benefits from both fuel types.

Some of the benefits of E85, over conventional gasoline powered vehicles, include the potential for localised production of fuel in agricultural areas. Another benefit is the potentially reduced level of pollution in the earth's atmosphere, especially CO_2. Hence, E85 can play a key role in reducing the effects of global warming. According to latest research, E85 is being used extensively in North America and several parts of Europe.

I see no reason why we should be lethargic in adopting proven, path-breaking technologies. In fact, I have discussed the need to devise ethanol engines suited to Indian needs with India's leading automobile manufacturers. If tractors and jeeps in rural India can run on ethanol, then farmers can meet their own fuel consumption needs. Even otherwise, as against the cost of ₹65 or 70 per litre of normal fuel, I am confident that ethanol can be made available at not more than ₹20 per litre.

In conclusion, I just wish to say that the vast benefits of biofuel are difficult to ignore: Reduction in the price of petroleum products, pollution abatement, employment to farmers and tribal welfare. All these will improve our economy. Yet, in these last nine years, the UPA government has done precious little on this front.

I would strongly recommend that a separate ministry is created for biotechnology. Only then can one expect some serious initiatives on this front. I am, however, happy to note the initiatives of BJP in this regard. We have set up our own biotechnology cell which is constantly studying ways and means to spread awareness and promote biofuel. The need of the hour is for people to be more aware about the subject. Their informed choice will serve our economy a great deal.

Overcoming India's Electricity Deficit: Exploring Alternatives

While water is a natural resource, electricity is purely man-made. However, after water, if there is something that holds critical importance in today's life, it is electricity. The two, put together, are the biggest determinants of a society's social progress.

I recall that when I was a kid, electricity was a metaphor for national aspiration. We valued electricity because we believed that the day it reaches our homes, it would illuminate our lives and end all our problems. As years went by, its erratic availability and load-shedding notwithstanding, electricity did reach vast sections of our population. However, even today, approximately 300 million people in our country have no access to electricity. So, when the sun sets for 25 per cent of our population, their lives are engulfed in darkness till the sun rises the next morning.

I have dwelt upon the problem of water management in detail. It is important to have a clear plan to overcome India's electricity deficit as it is impeding the growth of our nation. As of July 2013, India's electricity deficit is a mere 5700 MW i.e. 4.5 per cent against demand. However, as in several other cases, the figure is misleading and does not quite reflect the gravity of the problem.

Absence of electricity in villages defeats the attempts to spread education there. Absence of education results in continued unemployment, which in turn results in continued and unabated poverty. At the same time, electricity shortage in urban areas results in reduced and inconsistent electricity supply to industrial units which adversely impacts their productivity.

The solution to the energy crisis in our country can be found if we follow a two-pronged approach. As I have advocated in other cases, we must not depend upon the government alone. We must understand the true import of the statement: *After God and Government, there is you.* Private entrepreneurs, who are capable, should set up electricity plants. Enhanced production, even if it is scattered, will add up to the whole.

If the government seriously explores alternate means of electricity generation, it will prove to be a crucial step in bridging the rising deficit in the present-day context. The conventional way of depending largely upon coal is not doing us much good, what with our coal reserves getting scarce. The government, thus, ought to devise a long-term plan, giving the right importance to alternative sources, which have, so far, only played a peripheral role.

I would like to refer to a paper published by DV Kapur, founder-chairman of the National Thermal Power Corporation (NTPC), in the Observer Research Foundation (ORF) journal, *ORF Discourse*. According to this paper, 'All-India generation capacity of utilities (excluding captive units) has increased from 1,713 MW in 1951 to 163,670 MW including 16,429 MW in renewable sources as on 31 July 2010. This is split into 80,775 MW in the state sector, 51,728 MW in central sector and 31,167 MW in private sector. Mode-wise the present installed capacity consists of thermal: 105,647 MW (coal: 87,093 MW, gas: 17,354 MW, diesel: 1,200 MW), hydro: 37,033 MW, nuclear: 4,560 MW and renewable energy sources: 16,429 MW.'

Now, given the present deficit, the challenge here is to increase this production capacity by 12-13 per cent. And to explore how this can be done, we will need to dissect the production of electricity from various different sectors.

Coal is the most important fuel for India's power sector. It is the source of more than 70 per cent of generating capacity. But, coal shortages, delays in its transportation and the low thermal quality of coal supplies cause disruptions in power generation and result in lower plant productivity. All these also result in increasing the cost.

Therefore, it makes sense to explore alternatives to coal. As I have mentioned before, I experimented with generating electricity from bagasse. Thus, cogeneration plants carry their own advantages where the by-products obtained from one manufacturing unit can be utilised in the manufacturing process of the other product.

Similarly, electricity can also be produced from rice husk. Rice hulls (or rice husks) are the hard protecting coverings of rice grains. With proper techniques, rice hulls can be burned and used to power steam engines. This presents a massive opportunity to all those states which are rich in rice farming.

In 2007, a group of four friends began a massive exercise to produce electricity from rice husk in Bihar. Husk Power Systems is an impressive initiative by these youngsters, providing the cheapest way to address electricity woes in the poverty-stricken state. When rice is milled, the outside kernel, or husk, is discarded. Because the husk contains a lot of silica, it is not suitable for cooking. A recent Greenpeace study reports that Bihar alone produces 1.8 billion kg of rice husk per year. Most of it ends up rotting in landfills and emitting methane, a greenhouse gas. Husk Power Systems has come up with a method that can burn

50 kg of rice husk in an hour, which generates 32 KW—sufficient for about 500 families living in rural areas.

The electricity thus produced is very cheap. Often the cost is lesser than what a rural household spends on kerosene, whereas the light is brighter and eco-friendly. This initiative only reiterates the power of innovative thinking. Rice is India's pre-eminent crop and the staple food of the people in the eastern and southern parts of the country. There are at least eight states that are extremely conducive to rice farming, including Andhra Pradesh, which tops the list, West Bengal and Tamil Nadu. If electricity production from rice husk were to be explored in an organised, well-planned manner in these states, India's electricity deficit can be vastly reduced.

India has the fifth largest installed wind power capacity in the world. In 2009-10 India's growth rate was amongst the top four countries in the world. As on 31 December 2010, the installed capacity of wind power in India was 13,065.37 MW, mainly spread across Tamil Nadu (4,906.74 MW), Maharashtra (2,077.70 MW), Gujarat (1,863.64 MW), Rajasthan (1,088.37 MW), Andhra Pradesh (136.05 MW), Kerala (27.75 MW) and Odisha (2 MW). Wind power accounts for 6 per cent of India's total installed power capacity, and it generates 1.6 per cent of the country's power.

Even when I was the president of the Maharashtra BJP, I had advocated installing windmills in the sea, as these could generate over 4,000 MW of electricity every year. Another reason why wind energy needs to be promoted is because its zero emissions will go a long way in reducing CO_2 presence in the environment. Another source that needs to be tapped more proactively is solar energy. For this, the government must provide incentives to solar cell manufacturing units. Efforts ought to be made to reduce the cost of manufacturing, which in turn will reduce the cost of the electricity thus produced.

I would also take this opportunity to laud the efforts of an NGO called the Barefoot College, which has been a pioneer in solar electrification in rural, remote, non-electrified villages since 1989. These efforts have gone a long way in improving the lives of villagers in several districts of Rajasthan.

Then comes the issue of nuclear energy. It is a given fact that if we have to sustain the high growth rate of GDP, then, at some point, availing nuclear energy will become an imperative. However, the challenge here lies in setting up these plants judiciously so that they do not cause damage to the environment. These concerns have obviously been underlined by the recent disaster in Japan.

The meltdown at the Fukushima Daiichi nuclear power plant in Okuma, Japan, in the aftermath of the earthquakes and tsunami in March 2011, has raised fresh questions over human safety, especially in areas in the vicinity of these plants. The radiation exposure is bound to have serious repercussions on the health of people living in those areas. We must see this crisis as a wake-up call for us. In setting up nuclear plants in India, utmost care ought to be taken to ensure that all potential concern areas, be it location of the plant or its technical aspects are duly addressed. Besides, a proper plan needs to be in place to rehabilitate the villagers, if at all their lands are acquired to set up a nuclear plant.

Last but not the least, my concern remains the poorest of the poor. On one of my visits to Uttarakhand, an idea struck me. In vast jungle stretches in Uttarakhand and elsewhere, leaves from felled trees are burnt to generate fire. Research has shown that burning of dried tree leaves can provide us a good secondary fuel source for power plants. We must provide the right set-up and know-how in rural areas to generate electricity in this manner. This can go a long way in improving conditions in some of the least privileged tribal areas.

Having dwelt upon the ways to overcome our electricity deficit, I would like to take this opportunity to suggest something more radical. In the coming years, we must strive not only to overcome our electricity deficit but also produce surplus electricity. When that happens, we must draw inspiration from Israel and set up a massive electric car network in all our major cities.

On a visit to Israel, I was amazed to see the breakthroughs achieved by the country in this direction. With the support of Israel's government, Israeli-American entrepreneur Shai Agassi's company has proposed a radical solution to the country's fuel problems. They are wiring Israel with tens of thousands of spots where electric cars can plug in and recharge. Steps are also being taken to construct roadside recharge stations where batteries can be replaced, to facilitate people who have to go on a longer trip. The batteries will be swapped for recharged ones in less than five minutes. Software developed by the company will send cars to the nearest charging point—and manage the demand that these cars will put on the power grid.

Only a revolutionary long term plan like this can provide us a permanent solution from the damage that increasing fuel costs cause to the individual and to the country's economy. Besides, if electric cars become a reality in India, our expenditure on import of crude oil will decrease drastically. We can then invest the money, thus saved, into our infrastructure and irrigation projects, which will also generate vast employment opportunities.

I slept and dreamt that life was joy. I woke up and saw that life was service. I acted and behold, service was joy.

—Rabindranath Tagore

EIGHT

The Way Ahead

Charting the Future for the Individual and the Party

Before I dwell upon the future, it makes sense to think of ways to correct some of the fallacies of the present. One of the biggest problems that I have encountered in recent times is to cope with a slightly flawed understanding of politics that I see in many of the present-day political workers. As in other fields, politics too has not remained unaffected by consumerist influences.

So, instead of spending time in their local areas and sweating it out on streets and villages, many politicians think that by thronging to New Delhi at the slightest behest and hobnobbing with the party bigwigs, they will be able to bargain respectable positions for themselves. This is not the idea of politics I subscribe to and this is not the political culture I will ever encourage. I have told all my party workers to work in their local areas and not come to Delhi unless called or necessary. There is no reason why one must expect to get special treatment merely because of his or her proximity to leaders in Delhi. One needs to work his way up the ranks. That is the only way one can remain sensitive to the concerns of the disadvantaged.

Besides, I strongly believe that in a democracy, leaders occupying top positions ought to be elected, not nominated. Contesting elections makes them remain grounded and connected with the people of their respective constituencies. Leaders who have made it to the top without contesting elections are often unaware of people's problems. A case in point, as I have mentioned before, is Manmohan Singh, who despite being a Rajya Sabha MP from Assam for over two decades, has seldom spoken about the problems of the state.

When I became the BJP president, some people had suggested that I get myself nominated to the Rajya Sabha. However, I didn't want to take the easy route. I have decided to contest the Lok Sabha elections in 2014. It is my humble request to all top leaders of the BJP to contest the next Lok Sabha elections. When most leaders are elected from among the people, it will make our democracy stronger.

In my tenure as party president, I was aware that by merely setting rules and doling out a list of do's and don'ts, things will not work. After all, party workers are mature individuals and know what they are doing. What I did was, I set in motion a comprehensive performance appraisal plan wherein each party functionary's performance was evaluated on various parameters. The idea was to inspire a cultural change in the way we go about our politics.

When I speak of inspiring a cultural change, nothing can be a bigger change than our political workers reaching out to the poorest of the poor. It is with this objective in mind that I have always promoted *Antyodaya* so passionately.

As the BJP president, I had launched an innovative

campaign called the *Antyodaya Abhiyan*. Let me share with you, some facts about it. This campaign promotes politics for development through social work. We have asked all our party workers, our organisational units, as well as all our elected representatives, at every level, to take up at least one service (*sewa*) and development (*vikas*) project in their respective areas. Through this, our workers try and reach out effectively to the disadvantaged.

We have always believed that politics is an instrument for social and economic transformation. Therefore, all BJP members and activists are expected to make a resolution to reinstate the element of service in the political culture of this great nation. If one makes a determined effort, he or she can easily take up such activities and derive satisfaction from serving the last person in the queue. Even after quitting as party president, I have appealed to all party workers to pursue the *Antyodaya Abhiyan* with the same vigour.

In recent months, India has witnessed a massive movement against corruption. This movement, spearheaded by veteran social activist, Anna Hazare, brought out our civil society's angst against the government and, at times, against the political class per se. We must treat this as an opportunity to introspect and find out why we couldn't foresee such a movement taking shape. Is there indeed a growing disparity between the politicians and the people they are supposed to represent?

At my own level, I could sense this disparity and when I look back, one of the guiding thoughts behind my emphasis on *Antyodaya* was to bridge this gap. Besides, the greed for power often desensitises a human being, without him realising it. I felt that if a leader remains connected to the weakest sections of society, the sufferings of that world would help him remain more sensitive towards addressing them.

The key to *Antyodaya* at the public policy level is in enabling the economy to produce gainful and sustainable livelihoods. In the Indian context, it means that the test of success of economic growth is whether our agriculture and rural economy are so revitalised that productive employment and high quality of life are ensured in rural areas. We must admit that India has not passed this test. The huge and rapidly growing divide and disparities between cities and villages, is a matter of grave concern.

It is my firm belief that the best and most plausible way this disparity can be bridged is by the personal efforts of political workers. This explains my appeal to all party workers to undertake at least one service and development activity. From running a free legal aid centre to organising polio immunisation camps, from checking school drop-out rates to forming self-help groups for women—innumerable avenues are waiting for well meaning, patriotic and socially motivated individuals to come forward and provide action-oriented leadership. I am confident that once our workers take up such tasks, it will bring in a sea change in their attitude towards politics and nation building. I am equally happy to note that BJP-run state governments are actually moving towards realising the vision of *Antyodaya* with great zeal.

Gujarat has succeeded in supplying 24×7 power supply to all its villages. Its recent initiative of holding *Garib Kalyan Mela*s is also very commendable. In Madhya Pradesh, several schemes for empowering the girl child have achieved remarkable success. The BJP government in Karnataka was perhaps the first state government to have prepared a Vision 2020 plan and had also started implementing the same. The plan identified twelve key areas that will play a pivotal part in the overall progress of the state. Some of those areas were overall viability of agriculture, empowerment of local government, improving access to healthcare facilities in the state with the aim of serving every citizen, empowerment of women and enhancing job opportunities for them. The plan also focussed on developing tourism as an industry in the state, apart from concentrating on other important areas like the economical and educational empowerment of vulnerable groups and backward classes in the region. Even our minority government in Jharkhand, led by Arjun Munda, had launched a commendable scheme in July 2011 called 'Mukhya Mantri Dal Bhaat Yojana', that provided nutritious meals to the poor for just ₹5. This certainly should not make us complacent and we must further improve our performance in governance. If we come across some examples of good governance in non-BJP states, I am sure we will try to replicate them and strive for a quality transformation in our set up.

CAPACITY BUILDING

As party president, I had also begun some new initiatives within the party organisation. We had initiated a major nationwide campaign for building the capacities of our party workers, party functionaries and elected representatives at every level. Every party worker was expected to participate in the three-phased training programmes and serve the party in a more result-oriented manner. Comprehensive syllabi for all major sections of party rank and file had been drafted.

We had also launched e-training programmes. It must be stated here that, while selecting party workers for shouldering responsibilities, their ability and their capacity to deliver the goods ought to be given more importance and, hence, it makes sense to get trained and build our capacities. Training helps improve performance in every sphere.

In an unorganised profession like politics, it holds even

greater importance. I am sure a trained worker's productivity will be higher than the untrained one's.

We had initiated the process of setting up a comprehensive apparatus to review the performance of all our party office bearers at various levels: Elected representatives, MPs and MLAs and even ministers. Meritocracy ought to prevail in the present day and age. We had planned to institute awards at the national level for the best performing MP, MLA or MLC and even municipal councillor and a Sarpanch. This was needed to send the right signal, that performance gets rewarded, leading to some inspiration for non-performers as well. As I have indicated earlier, performance ought to be the key to an individual's progress in our party. As party president, I had asked all our party organisational units as well as elected representatives and even governments to prepare their own Annual Performance Reports. This exercise was aimed at promoting greater accountability and the party organisation would have got a chance to assess performances at various levels.

The importance of technology in today's day and age cannot be emphasised enough. We should use all available modern communication technologies to galvanise our party. However, we do know the limitations of technology and nothing can replace person to person contact. In the next few years, we are committed to reaching out to the younger generation through the avenues they commonly frequent and, through technology, provide them a vehicle for their political participation.

Generating newer employment opportunities for the youth has been and will continue to be an area of thrust for us. I had, thus, urged all our state governments to revisit their youth development policies and come up with programmes with greater emphasis on employability enhancement of the youth.

I take pride in the fact that while there are many women-led political parties, BJP is the only party that has 33 per cent reservation for women within the organisation.

But quotas alone are not enough. Men in politics must change their mindset and ensure that women are given greater scope and are helped in every way for their own empowerment. Our society will be empowered when women are empowered.

In the sphere of public policy as well as party organisation, nationalism, development, poverty alleviation, ethical values and discipline would be the cornerstones of our positions. We must strive to develop a culture of cohesiveness in the organisation. We must remember that we are seen, very rightly, as a party with conventional values and ethics and it would not be proper for us to tolerate any form of corruption anywhere. Indiscipline is another evil which I dealt with very firmly. There are always differences of opinion within a party. There is also a right forum to raise these differences. Intra-party discussions cannot happen via the media.

In my tenure as president, I had always stressed on the importance of good governance, as an essential instrument that not only enhances the credibility of the party, but helps in winning elections. We are the first and the only party that has a good governance cell, dedicated to provide all assistance to our governments to improve their performance. The Chief Minister of Goa, Manohar Parrikar, is the convener of this cell. I am happy that in June 2010, a *Suraj Sankalp* convention was held under the auspices of this cell in Mumbai. At this convention, we had once again committed ourselves to what is now being described as 'people-oriented, pro-active good governance' (p2g2). All the chief ministers and deputy chief ministers from the BJP-ruled states, besides over sixty ministers belonging to eight states along with some senior party functionaries in the states as well as at the Centre, had participated in this two-day convention held at the Rambhau Mhalgi Prabodhini on the outskirts of Mumbai. This convention was the first of its kind and the *Suraj Sankalp* or the declaration of determination that we adopted reflects our resolve to provide governance with a difference. Over the last few years, different news channels in India have invariably nominated chief ministers from the BJP-ruled states amongst the best chief ministers in the country. This is a matter of pride for us. Today, I can say this with a fair degree of satisfaction that people are no longer willing to buy our opponents' false propaganda against us. The citizens of our country acknowledge that we provide better administration than any other party. This will help us in a big way as we prepare for the 2014 Lok Sabha elections.

MILESTONES

Allow me to highlight a few milestones achieved in the various states where we have been in power directly or with an alliance partner. The national average of agricultural growth is only 2 per cent, while in Gujarat, it is several times above the same. In fact, in Gujarat, it has been consistently 9.5 per cent since 2002. In this era of environmental consciousness, our government in Himachal had made great strides and earned carbon points which certified their effective management. The government in Chhattisgarh has set a benchmark by accomplishing an impressive use of technology to make their Public Distribution System (PDS) transparent, while performing efficiently.

In my tenure as party president, I had travelled across the country from Chennai to Chandigarh and Guwahati to Goa. I met not only our party workers but also interacted with several opinion makers and prominent citizens wherever I went. From my experience, I can say there is a groundswell of good wishes for the BJP. We have supporters in every section and strata of society. Crores of countrymen have great hopes from all of us. They want the BJP to keep its distinct identity intact.

To be cynical is easy. Those who give up their efforts of being different, or making a great difference, lack the courage of conviction. We are all optimists but our optimism is not and cannot be just a pious hope. We must plan our path to make the BJP accomplish its historic mission. Some thirty-eight years ago, Delhi had heard the slogan, *Singhasan khali karo ki janata aayee hai* (*Vacate the throne, as the people have arrived*). Although this slogan was raised in Delhi, it had its origins in Patna, in the movement led by Jayaprakash Narayan. Three-and-a-half decades later, if we look around, we have a different kind of Emergency which is the result of misgovernance at the Centre. Once again, we have to raise our voices and ask the UPA government to either perform or perish.

In condemning the present government at the Centre for its multitudinous failures, we also need to be constantly aware of how our vision for the country differs from theirs. And clarity on that front can be achieved if we draw up a comprehensive vision plan for the country—the way we see India shaping up by 2025.

I believe that India has all the resources, natural as well as human, to grow to its full potential. We can indeed create a better tomorrow, with our own resources, to provide education for all, healthcare for all, housing for all, employment for all, and a better future for all the billion-plus people of India. If this has not been possible so far, it is due to lack of good policies and good governance. However, it is not enough for the BJP to just criticise others for following wrong policies; rather, we should take the lead in presenting superior policies. We should not just talk about the problems before the nation, but be in the vanguard of offering practical and effective solutions.

With this in mind, I had constituted a group of party workers and supporters to prepare an India Vision 2025 document. The group comprised senior leaders of the party who had served in important positions in the Central government, serving and former chief ministers and ministers in state governments, MPs, MLAs and mayors, as well as domain experts who are sympathisers of the BJP. In constituting this group, care had been taken to ensure the representation of a wide section of interests.

We must leave no stone unturned in reaching out to the underprivileged sections of society such as the Scheduled Castes (SCs), Scheduled Tribes (STs), Other Backward Classes (OBCs) and minorities in a big way. People are waiting for political workers who would respond to their agonies and aspirations. They are keen to join us, provided we connect with them. We must make a collective resolve to increase our vote share at least by 10 per cent, by breaking new ground and taking up new initiatives. Most importantly, we need to make ourselves acceptable to those sections of society which still have misconceptions about us. Effective communication and relentless reaching out is the only way we can address this problem.

We must remember that India cannot become a superpower just because we all want her to be. We will have to work hard for the transformation. We will have to revisit our objective for being in public life. Why should we seek inspiration only from getting a party post, a ticket in the elections or a berth in the ministry? Can we not derive inspiration from the higher purpose and power of politics—such as the desire to bring a smile to the faces of underprivileged brethren; to end the distress that has forced thousands of farmers to commit suicide; to eliminate the malnutrition that is killing tens of thousands of tribal children; to create employment opportunities for our talented youth? Isn't the goal of making India a strong nation, powerful enough to motivate us?

The path ahead is not easy for us. It is full of challenges, some of which I have tried to highlight here. We should neither expect quick success, nor work with that motive alone. We should neither get disheartened by temporary setbacks, nor get overjoyed by immediate achievements. Our yardstick of success is how much and how fast we move in the direction of making India achieve all-round progress and regain her glory and greatness.

Our vision is to build an India that is free of hunger, fear and corruption, and also free of inequality and injustice of all kinds. We want to build a nation that is self-reliant, capable and can achieve the impossible. We want to build an India that has peace and harmony within and strives ceaselessly for peace and harmony in the entire world; an India whose ancient intellectual and material prowess, cultural light, civilisational genius and spiritual force is revived and taken to unprecedented heights. We must have the confidence that the twenty-first century, undisputedly, is that of India, our great Bharat Mata!

E-GOVERNANCE

It is our strong belief that one of the best ways to bring about qualitative changes in our standards of governance is by employing e-governance to ensure transparency and accountability in the working of the government. A well planned e-governance strategy can build a more efficient, citizen-centric India. E-governance not only allows efficient accessibility of services to the common man, it provides a platform for citizen empowerment and participation in the governance process, leading to citizen satisfaction and overall reduction in corruption.

The BJP considers e-governance as a potent tool to combat corruption in our country. Hence, our government in Gujarat has undertaken massive e-governance initiatives to bridge the gap between the government and the citizen. Having said that, we would like to acknowledge and learn from the initiatives undertaken in this direction by non-BJP governments as well. In fact, in 2010, we had sent a team to study some of the path-breaking initiatives undertaken in this direction by the Congress-led government in Andhra Pradesh.

For effective implementation of e-governance, it will need to be classified into five verticals:

1. **Digital data and e-records:** The main source of corruption is the non-availability of information to the common man. This information is often buried in files and papers that are not accessible to the common citizen. If this information is digitised, with the help of new technologies, including the web, anyone can access the same. This will go a long way in eliminating malpractices and corruption. I must add here that while some states like Gujarat, Chhattisgarh and Karnataka have taken vast strides in this direction, several other states have a lot of catching up to do. The BJP government in Karnataka had, to a great extent, been able to eliminate the undue influences of village accountants in manipulating land titles and land transfers by introducing the BHOOMI project. Similarly, Gujarat has e-Dhara, which offers administrative information to the remote villages. Madhya Pradesh has Bhu-Abhilekha which offers similar services. An ideal situation would be when every state in India accomplishes full digitisation of all government records. Hence, land records, property registration, property tax assessment, vehicle registration, passport, etc. can be digitised and made available to the common man.
2. **E-delivery:** One of the most important factors in

successful deployment of e-governance is its delivery to the common man. A lot has been said and written about this. However, except for a few states like Gujarat, Madhya Pradesh, Chhattisgarh, Andhra Pradesh etc., very little has been done in this regard. The major focus for delivery of e-governance in the present system is on information kiosks. However, considering the poor computer literacy percentage in our country, a large number of manned workstations are required in every panchayat. Thus manned kiosks have been proposed as an alternative. The Madhya Pradesh government has initiated a programme called 'MP Online' which is a good start in this direction. The programme aims to provide all important services to its citizens online. Thus, applying for driving licenses and passports, downloading forms for entrance exams to government colleges etc. can now be done easily with the help of this initiative.

3. **E-procurement/e-tendering:** Government procurement is a major source of corruption. By using e-procurement process and introducing appropriate tender criteria—bribes, kickbacks and cartelisation can be fought to a great extent.
4. **E-monitoring:** This can prove to be a major tool to combat corruption. New technologies such as biometric identification and GSM technologies, combined with effective implementation of the AADHAR/UID project, can be used to monitor various schemes. The effective monitoring of the PDS system in Chhattisgarh and the National Rural Employment Guarantee Act (MGNREGA) in Andhra Pradesh using GPS, biometric and mobile technologies has

led to reduction in leakages in the system, resulting in efficient delivery and higher citizen satisfaction.

5. **Performance management:** It is the first step towards improving performance. A comprehensive workflow management system can lead to internal accountability of all departments and better access to work/task status. Since 2005, Gujarat has implemented the Integrated Workflow and Document Management System (IWDMS). This is an effective workflow management system, a one of its kind system in India, leading to a very high level of internal efficiency and accountability of government employees.

A Study of Exemplary Development Policies Implemented in Various States

Commitment to good governance ought to be enhanced through innovative schemes and policies. All our state governments have shown remarkable foresight in approaching this task. These state governments have initiated some exceptionally pro-active policies in the last few years. These policies have varied in their objectives—from fulfilling irrigation needs, to encouraging education of the girl child and even to introducing e-governance in some of the most sluggish departments of the government.

The results are there for everybody to see. Chhattisgarh has bagged a gold medal in e-governance for making PDS online in the state. Various initiatives of the Gujarat government are being emulated by Congress-ruled state governments. The fact that Congress leaders are still not willing to face the truth about Gujarat's development prevents them from acknowledging the same. The girl child empowerment scheme launched by the government in Madhya Pradesh has brought a radical change in people's approach towards educating the girl child.

Good governance essentially comprises path-breaking initiatives like these which undo the ineffectiveness of existing policies. Given the fact that I personally keep myself updated on the status of development policies in BJP-ruled states, I will, for obvious reasons, be able to speak about them more exhaustively. However, I feel just as elated when I am informed about any other effective development project in any other state. In fact, it is my personal belief that path-breaking initiatives need to be emulated, irrespective of who promotes them.

One such scheme which has impressed me is the Biju Gram Jyoti Yojana, launched by the Odisha government. This scheme, launched in 2007, essentially focuses on electrification of habitations or villages (wherever electrification is feasible through grid connectivity i.e. conventional electricity) with a population of less than 100 people as per the 2001 Census. A maximum cost limit of ₹3.5 lakh per habitation/village (to be limited to actual) has been outlined for this purpose. This scheme has played a pivotal role in improving conditions in the most backward regions of Odisha.

There's another scheme of the Odisha government that deserves appreciation—the Utkal Sabuj Gram Yojana. Launched in 2005, this scheme is for wasteland development, a subject very close to my heart. There are five broad objectives of this scheme:

1. Take up plantation in wastelands within Gram Panchayat areas.
2. Meet the demand of timber and bamboo for construction of houses of beneficiaries belonging to BPL families.
3. Generate income for the Gram Panchayat, by selling the crop of fruit-bearing plants and other minor forest produce, including bamboo and fuelwood.

4. Encourage people to go in for plantation in their own and community lands.
5. Prevent soil erosion.

The integrated approach and comprehensive planning of this scheme gives a big boost not just to wasteland reclamation but also to poverty alleviation.

In 2009, the Andhra Pradesh government launched a scheme called Polambadi, which covers the area of farmers' training. Under this scheme, farmers are provided training for use of eco-friendly measures (bioagents and biopesticides) for control of crop pests which, in turn, reduce cost of cultivation and improve the quality of produce, resulting in high market price and good returns. I do believe that such a scheme, if launched at a national level, will yield very positive results, thereby improving the overall agricultural economy.

Apart from these, it gives me immense pride to share with you, some of the initiatives undertaken by BJP governments in three different states. In choosing these initiatives that I am sharing with you here, out of the hundreds, my criterion was to pick out those, which in my opinion, have left the maximum impact on improving governance and, correspondingly, the quality of life of people in these states. That, by no means, should suggest that the other states have done any less. On the other hand, dwelling upon these three states should serve as a case study on how overall dynamism and decisiveness towards ushering in new schemes across the country can catapult India to a different league.

GUJARAT—ELECTRICITY, WATER

When it comes to Gujarat, one has a tough time deciding which scheme to pick out for a special mention and which to leave out. And the reason is simple. Gujarat is way ahead of all states in all aspects of development: Electricity generation, irrigation, e-governance, public health, SEZs, etc.

Solar Power: On 20 April 2012, Gujarat created history when Chief Minister Narendra Modi dedicated over 600 MW of installed solar power projects to the nation. The projects, having a potential to generate 30 lakh units of clean energy per day, are spread over several districts. These include Asia's largest solar park with 214 MW generation capacity at a village in the north Gujarat district of Patan. The park at Charanka, spread across 5,000 acres, has 500 MW of generation capacity of both solar and wind energy. Leading solar project developers like Alex Astral, US-based Sun Edison, Lanco Solar, Roha Dyechem and GMR Gujarat Solar Power have set up plants in the park.

While 214 MW of grid connected solar power was commissioned at Charanka by 17 national and international companies, 10 solar plants having a combined generation capacity of 87.49 MW have gone on stream in Surendranagar, 8 in Kutch (85 MW) and 3 each in Banaskantha (55.20 MW) and Rajkot (25MW), amongst others. As Modi himself has put it, this is a major step towards achieving India's energy security. What is equally significant is that Gujarat being an energy surplus state, mass production of solar energy will lead to a shift towards green energy which will address some of India's major environmental concerns as well.

Swagat: Also noteworthy is the advances made by Gujarat in e-governance. The Chief Minister considered the enormous scope of IT to address public grievances, on the lines of e-governance being used by other states, to introduce administrative reforms.

He introduced an innovative programme called Swagat in 2006, which enables direct communication between the citizens and the Chief Minister, thus, making Gujarat the first state to introduce this kind of a facility for its citizens. In Gandhinagar, the fourth Thursday of every month is a Swagat day, wherein the highest officer in administration attends to the grievances of the man on the street. Grievances are logged in, transmitted and made available online to the officers concerned who have to reply within three to four hours. The departments concerned then have to be ready with the replies, before 3 p.m., when the Chief Minister holds video conferences with all the districts concerned. Applicants are called one by one and the Chief Minister examines each complaint in detail. The information sent by the department is also reviewed online in the presence of the complainant and the Collector/District Development Officer/Superintendent of Police and other officials concerned. Attempts are made to offer a fair and acceptable solution on the same day and no applicant has ever left without any firm reply to his grievance. The record is then preserved in the Swagat database and a separate log is maintained for each case.

Swagat has provided the common man with an easy platform to get justice. The initiative taken by the Chief Minister has been lauded nationally and internationally, enriching many studies on how to make democracy more efficient. Gujarat's structured administration, the e-governance department's transparency with accountability and its successful strategies and experiments with technology have attracted the attention of top administrative officials in the entire nation. Owing to the innovative use of technology that injects accountability into government machinery, international institutions such as the Commonwealth Telecom Organisation and the University of Manchester have considered Swagat as an excellent model of e-transparency.

Health Management: In India, the government healthcare mechanism is another area that is fraught with irregularities and unprofessionalism. The Health Management Information System (HMIS) project was conceptualised and launched by the Gujarat government's Department of Health and Family Welfare in 2006 to ensure quality healthcare through the application of IT. The aim was to provide standard clinical and diagnostic tools, hospital management tools and integration of management information at the state level, thereby allowing online review and monitoring.

HMIS has been envisaged to not only help the administrators to have better monitoring and control of the functioning of hospitals across the state, using decision support indicators, but also assist doctors and medical staff to improve health services with readily available patient data for reference, work flow enabled paperless process and parameterised alarms and triggers during patient treatment cycle. HMIS enables the monitoring of pre-defined health indicators and the embedded exceptional reporting facilitates decision-making by the hospital management and state level administrators for policy and strategic decisions. This state-of-the-art healthcare solution, is aimed to provide better care to patients by addressing all the major functional areas of the hospital and the entire gamut of hospital activities.

Health is a sector which most governments in India tend to take for granted, when this is an area that calls for maximum attention, as human life is directly affected by it. With the HMIS initiative, the Gujarat government has once again set an example for other state governments in the country. While we focus on industrial plans and agricultural innovations, the need for similar radical upgradation in the social sector cannot be ignored.

Kalpasar: Irrigation and water management is another sector where the Gujarat government has taken a clear lead over other states.

Gujarat has embarked upon an ambitious project termed Kalpasar—which literally means a lake that fulfils wishes. Estimated to cost about ₹54,000 crore, this project envisages the construction of a dam of 64 km across the Gulf of Khambhat, joining River Ghogha on the west coast and River Hansot on the east coast of the Gulf, forming a water basin of more than 2,000 sq km. Through a 660 km canal system, 1.05 million hectares of land in coastal Saurashtra will be irrigated. The water will be available for domestic, agricultural and industrial use. In addition, Kalpasar is expected to generate 5,880 MW of tidal power. The project will have the potential to completely change the economic profile of the state.

We need out-of-the-box ideas and giant sized water projects in every state if we have to get rid of our water woes forever.

When it comes to electricity generation, the Jyoti Gram

Yojana of the Gujarat government, which was unveiled by the then Indian President, APJ Abdul Kalam in November 2006, has helped in improving the quality of life among the rural poor. From an earlier power supply situation of eight to fourteen hours a day, the Jyoti Gram Yojana, through its twenty-four-hour, high quality power, has given a tremendous boost to the rural economy. What is also unique about this initiative is the time-bound approach of this project. Implemented in a record time of thirty months, the Jyoti Gram Yojana has enabled Gujarat to become the first state in India to achieve 100 per cent electrification of villages.

Households, commercial establishments and educational institutions in these rural areas are now truly empowered and Jyoti Gram Yojana is a catalyst, helping to give a fillip to many socio-economic and educational revolutions.

Gujarat has always managed its power situation very well. The current power generating capacity of 9,700 MW (excluding 4,000 MW of captive generation) will be augmented to 15,000 MW in the next 5 years. The state government is also focussing on tapping non-conventional energy sources such as wind and tidal power and has also started commercial production of biodiesel. The state government has already declared incentive schemes for biogas-based cogeneration, energy generation through solar photo voltaic cells, geothermal sources, urban solid waste and biomass. Major new generation capacities are being added by harnessing wind energy, hydro-power, as well as through setting up gas and lignite-based power plants.

MADHYA PRADESH—EMPOWERING THE GIRL CHILD

It is my firm belief that the status of women in a society has a direct bearing on the status of society. This is because the outlook of women in a family influences the outlook of their children, which in turn affects the outlook of future generations. Hence, the most progressive and well educated families are those whose preceding generations encouraged their women towards education.

Unfortunately, even today, the level of education of the girl child in rural areas is very low. Hence, effective schemes that address this problem deserve to be applauded. One such scheme which has been very effective is the Madhya Pradesh government's scheme, launched on the initiative of Chief Minister Shivraj Singh Chouhan in 2007. It has gained tremendous popularity. Its success has been lauded by the entire nation. States like Uttar Pradesh and Delhi have also implemented the scheme.

Under the scheme, National Savings Certificate worth ₹6,000 is purchased in the name of the beneficiary girl consecutively for five years, that amounts to a total of ₹30,000. The girl is given ₹2,000 on getting admission in Class VI, ₹4,000 on admission in Class IX and ₹7,500 on being admitted to Class XI. After getting admission in Class XI, the girl is given ₹200 per month for the next two years. The rest of the amount, about ₹1.18 lakh in lump sum, will be given to her after attaining the age of twenty-one or appearing in Class XII exams, with the condition that the girl is married only after the age of eighteen years.

The state government, which is also leaving no stone unturned to give a legal shape to the scheme, has met with tremendous success in its implementation. It was the result of better and effective implementation of the scheme that people's concept about a girl's birth in their family changed completely, the rate of female foeticide came down appreciably and the sex ratio also got better, apart from improvement in the education and health status of girls in the state.

The state government, which is concerned about women's empowerment and a better future for girls, has been reviewing the scheme for further betterment. Shivraj Singh Chouhan has also been taking personal interest in the scheme's implementation and reviews it from time to time. The success of the girl child education scheme reiterates the importance of such social programmes that have the potential to revolutionise the quality of life and mindset of our rural population.

CHHATTISGARH—PUBLIC DISTRIBUTION SYSTEM

As I have mentioned before, the digitisation of the PDS in Chhattisgarh was a path-breaking step towards using technology to fight corruption. In July 2007, the Food and Civil Supplies department of the Government of Chhattisgarh took up the challenging task of implementing an end-to-end computerisation of paddy procurement, under the Minimum Support Price (MSP) and the PDS in July 2007. The project covers nearly 1,500 paddy procurement centres in remote villages and over 200 offices and warehouses of the Food Department, Chhattisgarh State Civil Supplies Corporation (CGSCSC), Chhattisgarh State Cooperative Marketing Federation (Markfed), Food Corporation of India (FCI), State Warehousing Corporation (SWC) and Central Warehousing Corporation (CWC) in all eighteen districts of the state. This radical step has ended many of the evils of the previous system and ushered in a paradigm shift in the rural economy of Chhattisgarh.

To list some of the benefits of this initiative:

- The system provides automatic calculation and release of monthly allotment of PDS schemes to 10,400 fair price shops.
- Under the project, all existing ration cards were cancelled and fresh, coded and bar-coded ration cards were issued to 37 lakh BPL families. This eliminated nearly 3 lakh fake ration cards. As the entire database of ration cards with family details and entitlement data is available in the public domain on the department's website, it has led to the whole system

becoming transparent. In the process, corruption has almost been weeded out of the system.

- A massive inventory management infrastructure and prompt disbursement of payment to paddy producing farmers are the other benefits of this system.

According to an article published in *The Hindu* on 18 November 2010, titled, 'The PDS turnaround in Chhattisgarh':

> ...Today, close to 80 per cent of the rural population—including all SC/ST households—is entitled to PDS grain at either one or two rupees per kilo. The fact that most rural households have a strong stake in the PDS has generated immense pressure on the system (ration shops in particular) to deliver. Expanded PDS coverage and lower issue prices have both contributed to enhancing the voice of otherwise poor and disempowered rural cardholders. Another major reform was to ensure "doorstep delivery" of the PDS grain. This means that grain is delivered by state agencies to the ration shop each month, instead of dealers having to lift their quotas from the nearest godown. How does this help? It is well known that corrupt dealers have a tendency to give reduced quantities to their customers and sell the difference in the black market (or rather the open market). What is less well understood is that the diversion often happens before supplies reach the village. Dealers get away with this by putting their hands up helplessly and telling their customers that "*picche se kam aaya hai*" (there was a shortfall at the godown). When the grain is delivered to the ration shop, in the village, it is

> much harder for the dealers to siphon it off without opposition. Truck movements from the godowns to the ration shops are carefully monitored and, if a transporter cheats, the dealers have an incentive to mobilise local support to complain, as we found had happened in one village.

It is no wonder that the Chhattisgarh model of computerised PDS management has become a benchmark for our country. Various state governments have shown an interest in replicating this system in their respective states, while some are in the process of implementing it. I feel happy and proud that the Chhattisgarh PDS system has helped in a big way in improving the conditions of the most-underprivileged and disadvantaged sections of society.

I can list several other successful schemes and policies of our state governments. I can say this with satisfaction, that these policies have improved the quality of life of the common man. They have helped us in living up to our commitment towards good governance.

In conclusion, as I reach the end of this thoroughly enjoyable journey of communicating with my readers, I wish to reiterate that India, today, is on the threshold of several positive, qualitative changes. The onus for precipitating those changes is on us. We must choose content over form. We must choose good governance over meek status quo.

This is the time when we, the people of this country, have to prepare ourselves to play a more proactive role in shaping not just our individual destinies but the collective destiny of our nation.

To quote from an exhortation used upon Brutus in Shakespeare's *Julius Caeser*:

> *There is a tide in the affairs of men, which taken*

> *at the flood, leads on to fortune. Omitted, all the voyage of their life is bound in shallows and in miseries. On such a full sea are we now afloat. And we must take the current when it serves, or lose our ventures.*

Given the sad state of affairs the UPA has gifted to the country, corrective action must be taken now or never. If we lose this opportunity, history will not judge us kindly.

I pray to God to give us strength.

Notes and References

Chapter 3 Engine of Growth

1. http://pibmumbai.gov.in/scripts/detail.asp?releaseId=E2009PR1415
2. http://infrastructure.gov.in/pdf/compendium-of-ppp-infrastructure.pdf

Chapter 5 Urban Infrastructure

1. http://www.nagpurmihan.com/

Chapter 6 Natural Resource Management

1. *Loksamwad*, Sept 2008, Nagpur Municipal Corporation's monthly newsletter.
2. http://dolr.nic.in/iwdp1.htm

Chapter 7 Green Energy

1. www.cbdacg.com/about.htm

Index